English for Human Resources

Pat Pledger

SHORT COURSE
SERIES

Autorin	Pat Pledger, Hamburg
kritische Durchsicht	Britta Landermann, Steinhagen
	Gabriela Berndt, Frankfurt am Main
Verlagsredaktion	Janan Barksdale
Redaktionelle Mitarbeit	Christine House, Louise Kennedy, Gabriela Berndt und Fritz Preuss (Wortliste), Sarah Smith
Bildredaktion	Uta Hübner
Gesamtgestaltung und technische Umsetzung	Sylvia Lang

Bild- und Textquellen

Titelfoto: Paul A. Souders/Corbis GmbH
Fotos: Banana Stock: S. 52; BilderBox: S. 45; Caro Fotoagentur: S. 12/Goettlicher; Comstock: S. 8, 12; Corel Library: S. 41 (2); Corbis GmbH: S. 36/B. Varie; F1ONLINE: S. 12/E. Prod; Getty Images: S. 5/RF, S. 10/R. Brimson, S. 14/RF, S. 23/S. Marks, S. 24/RF, S. 25/Fisher/Thatcher, S. 26/RF, S. 33/RF, S. 42/RF/G & M.D. de Lossy, S. 50/RF, S. 59/RF; STOCK4B: S. 12/U. Zintel; Zefa: S. 16/M. Salmeron, S. 20/P. Tremblay, S. 34/T. Hemmings (2)/J. Feingersh (2), S. 40/R. Morsch, S. 47/R. Gomez
Cartoons: Oxford Designers & Illustrators

Wir danken folgenden Institutionen für die freundliche Abdruckerlaubnis: S. 15: Virgin Atlantic Airways (Text und Logo); S. 50: IG Metall Vorstand, verdi Bundesverwaltung, Österreichischer Gewerkschaftsbund ÖGB

Nicht alle Copyright-Inhaber konnten ermittelt werden; deren Urheberrechte werden hiermit vorsorglich und ausdrücklich anerkannt.

Weitere Titel in der *Short Course Series*:

English for Accounting	978-3-464-01880-4
English for the Automobile Industry	978-3-464-01877-4
English for Customer Care	978-3-464-01882-8
English for Marketing and Advertising	978-3-464-01876-7
English for Meetings	978-3-464-01874-3

www.cornelsen.de

Die Internet-Adressen und -Dateien, die in diesem Lehrwerk angegeben sind, wurden vor Drucklegung geprüft (Stand: Februar 2005). Der Verlag übernimmt keine Gewähr für die Aktualität und den Inhalt dieser Adressen und Dateien oder solcher, die mit ihnen verlinkt sind.

1. Auflage, 2. Druck 2006 / 06

Alle Drucke dieser Auflage sind inhaltlich unverändert
und können im Unterricht nebeneinander verwendet werden.

© 2005 Cornelsen Verlag, Berlin

Druck: CS-Druck CornelenStürz, Berlin

ISBN 13: 978-3-464-1881-1
ISBN 10:   3-464-1881-4

 Inhalt gedruckt auf säurefreiem Papier aus nachhaltiger Forstwirtschaft.

Inhalt

Vorwort

English for Human Resources wurde speziell für Beschäftigte im Personalwesen entwickelt, für deren Arbeit Englischkenntnisse notwendig sind. Sowohl Leiter von Personalabteilungen und deren Mitarbeiter als auch Beschäftigte in Personalagenturen können mit diesem SHORT COURSE gezielt die Redewendungen und Vokabeln erlernen, die für eine effektive Kommunikation in englischer Sprache in ihrem Arbeitsbereich relevant sind.

English for Human Resources besteht aus sechs Units, die unterschiedliche Gebiete des Personalwesens behandeln. Jede Unit beginnt mit dem sogenannten Clock-in, das aus kurzen Übungen, *Brainstorming* oder einem Quiz besteht. Es folgen Dialoge, Texte und authentische Dokumente sowie eine Vielfalt von Übungen, die helfen, wichtige Vokabeln und Redewendungen im Kontext zu erlernen. In den Units wird jeweils verwiesen auf die Partner files im Anhang – *Information-gap*-Übungen in Form von Rollenspielen, die es Ihnen ermöglichen, den in der Unit erlernten Wortschatz in typischen Situationen mit einem Partner oder einer Partnerin zu trainieren.

In **English for Human Resources** geht es nicht nur um aktives Sprechen, sondern es werden auch Fachthemen behandelt. Jede Unit endet mit einem Clock-out-Text, der sich inhaltlich auf das Thema der Unit bezieht und zur Diskussion anregt. Best practice-Kästchen vermitteln Tipps und Redemittel für typische Personalaufgaben wie z. B. das Verfassen von Stellenbeschreibungen oder Einstellungsverträgen. Darüber hinaus bieten Did you know?-Kästchen zusätzliche landeskundliche und sprachliche Informationen.

Wenn alle Units bearbeitet sind, können Sie Ihren Kenntnisstand anhand eines Kreuzworträtsels überprüfen, mit dem das Vokabular des SHORT COURSE wiederholt wird – Test yourself!

Im Anhang von **English for Human Resources** finden Sie einen Answer Key, mit dem Sie Ihre Lösungen selbstständig überprüfen können. Der Anhang enthält außerdem die Partner files, eine A–Z word list sowie eine Sammlung von Model letters. Mit Hilfe der Zusammenstellung von Useful phrases and vocabulary können Sie auch am Arbeitsplatz die häufigsten Redewendungen schnell nachschlagen.

Recruitment

CLOCK-IN

Put the following list of recruitment tasks in the order you think they normally occur.

☐ a Check or write the job description.

☐ c Prepare a person specification.

☐ b Make a job offer.

☐ e Shortlist applicants from the first interviews.

☐ f Conduct second interviews.

☐ d Advertise the job.

☐ g Carry out screening and interviews.

☐ h Select the most suitable candidate.

[1] i After an employee resigns, analyze the job and consider alternatives for hiring a replacement (eg internal staff versus the labour market).

☐ j Send feedback to unsuccessful applicants.

Compare your results with a colleague's or check the key.
In the above example an employee resigns. Can you think of other reasons to look for new staff?
Which recruitment tasks above are you involved in?

1 **Job descriptions and person specifications are two important HR tools.**
What type of information do they include? Sort the items below into the chart.

~~desirable skills~~
previous experience
reporting relationship (who person is
   responsible to and for)
job title
practical requirements (shift work, travel, etc)

location of workplace
skills and qualities needed for job
main purpose of job
qualifications/training
key duties/responsibilities
personal style/behaviour

Job description	Person specification
	desirable skills

2 Label the sections of the job description extract below with section headings from the box.

> Essential experience • Job title • Key duties/responsibilities •
> Main purpose of job • Reports to • Responsible for • Workplace location

JOB DESCRIPTION

1 _____ Training Manager – UK

2 _____ General Manager, UK and Northern Europe

3 _____ A small team of UK trainers
2 administrators
1 secretary/personal assistant

4 _____ To design, develop and carry out general training programmes for UK-based personnel, with particular emphasis on IT and sales-related training. To work closely with branch managers on implementing team-building training and monitoring effectiveness.

5 _____ To design and implement new training courses and record results and to identify future needs of the company.

To prepare a staff training manual for use at all branch offices.

To carry out an initial training audit and prepare a report on findings with on-going suggestions.

To be responsible for the annual UK training budget, to report to the Board annually and to work within the agreed budget.

To visit all branch offices regularly in order to train branch managers, review on-going training and assess customer service.

To report weekly to the General Manager, UK & Northern Europe.

6 _____ Training management and evaluation experience.
Management and coordination of team of trainers.
Budget management.

7 _____ Based in Manchester, the job involves substantial travelling in Great Britain and Northern Ireland (eg to visit branch offices and carry out training programmes).

3 True or false? Correct the false statements.

1 The job is based in Northern Ireland and doesn't require much travelling.
2 The training manager is responsible for three people.
3 The job is for somebody with an extensive training background.
4 The training manager reports directly to the Board of Directors.
5 The training manager is responsible for conducting an audit of training requirements and preparing a new training manual.

BEST PRACTICE

The language of job descriptions
Keep job descriptions simple so that they are easy for job applicants to understand. Avoid complicated phrases, company jargon or abbreviations.
Below are some useful verbs to use when explaining key responsibilities:

to **develop** general training programmes
to **work** closely with branch managers
to **implement** new training courses
to **prepare** a staff training manual
to **carry out** an initial training audit
to **assess** customer service

Other verbs often used in job descriptions are:

to contribute	*beitragen*	to manage	*leiten*
to ensure	*gewährleisten*	to monitor	*kontrollieren*
to involve	*mit sich bringen*	to provide	*zur Verfügung stellen*
to maintain	*aufrechterhalten*	to support	*unterstützen*

Remember …
• people work **for** or **at** a company
• they work **in** a department or team
• they are responsible **for** other staff and **for** (doing) their work
• they are responsible **to** or accountable **to** their boss/manager

---

4 Choose the correct verbs to complete the sentences.

1 The training manager reports to/manages/monitors the general manager.
2 The suitable applicant must be able to develop/work/implement closely with branch offices and develop/introduce/support a good team spirit.
3 We need to contribute/implement/train new training courses and identify/develop/manage needs for the future development of the staff.
4 There is a certain amount of hands-on work which involves carrying out/ensuring/contributing training courses for UK-based personnel.
5 First you need to maintain/prepare/operate a new staff training manual.
6 UK branch offices need to be supported, so the job maintains/ensures/involves a lot of travelling.

5 **Complete the gaps with verbs from the list to describe some of the competencies of a manager. Try to use each verb once.**

> build • develop • ensure • identify • improve • motivate • react to

A manager should be able to:

_____ [1] staff performance.

_____ [2] an effective team.

_____ [3] change.

_____ [4] staff.

_____ [5] creativity.

_____ [6] problems.

_____ [7] deadlines are met.

6 **Use some of the verbs covered in this unit so far to write a short job description of your own job. Then swap job descriptions with a partner and discuss any improvements that could be made.**

7 **Now look at the person specification on the next page. It is for the training manager's position described on page 6. Work with a partner to decide where the section headings go.**

> Additional information • Skills and qualities needed for job • Desirable skills • Personal style/behaviour • Previous experience • Qualifications/training

8 **Match these words and phrases from the person specification with their definitions.**

☐ 1 to work on your own initiative

☐ 4 leadership

☐ 6 to coordinate

☐ 2 interpersonal skills

☐ 5 sound knowledge

☐ 7 training audit

☐ 3 open lines of communication

a   the ability to develop good relationships between yourself and others
b   to organize the different parts of an activity or the people involved so that everything works well
c   a careful examination to find out how much training is done and whether it is effective and necessary
d   creating and maintaining an atmosphere in which people communicate easily and effectively
e   to work independently, without anyone telling you what to do
f   a good level of information about or understanding of something
g   the ability to head a group or company

Person Specification
Training Manager – UK

1

Educated to degree level or equivalent experience
Institute of Training certificate
Language skills in French and German an advantage

2

At least five years' experience in a leadership/managerial training role in an IT or
a high-tech company
Member of recognized training organization(s)

3

Applicants must be able to demonstrate success in the following areas:
Managerial ability
Team building and ability to motivate staff
Creativity:
a) to identify future training needs
b) to design materials and manuals
c) to design and carry out training programmes
Preparation and implementation of training budgets and audits
Monitor staff performance throughout the organization
Maintain open lines of communication on all training issues with managers and
Board

4

Sound IT experience and knowledge of all general software programs
Customer care and quality management experience

5

Proven interpersonal skills
Ability to communicate at all levels of the organization
Active decision-maker able to work on own initiative
Innovative
Intercultural awareness and sensitivity
Team worker

6

Must be mobile and able to travel on a weekly basis.
This is a progressive role with opportunities for promotion in the US or Europe.

9 Now write a person specification for your own job and evaluate it with your colleagues.

10 Read the dialogue below between Jackie Branigan, head of HR at the UK head office of a large European manufacturing company, and David Grundy, her recruitment officer. What types of recruitment sources do they mention?

Jackie Good morning, David. How was your weekend?

David Excellent, thanks. Too short though!

Jackie Yes, I know what you mean. Can we just have a word about the search for the personnel officer in Berlin? I know that it's your responsibility, but I'd like to be up to date on what's happening.

David Well, the job description and person specification have both been finalized and cleared with Jürgen Müller in Berlin. We're looking for someone with 2–5 years' generalist HR experience, either an HR qualification or a degree and, last but not least, they must have high-level English skills.

Jackie So where are you planning to advertise?

David Well, firstly on our European intranet, although I don't think there's much chance of finding anybody in-house or in the European offices.

Jackie Not sure I agree with you there. Don't forget we took on a lot of employees with the merger in 2002 – there just might be some human resources potential there.

David Yes, you have a point there. Then I thought I'd put the vacancy with a couple of HR specialist recruitment consultancies which operate across Europe.

Jackie OK. What about an ad in the German HR trade paper? They have a monthly magazine, don't they?

David Yes, but there are very few job ads in there. I'll look into it though.

Jackie And where are you going to interview?

David Well, I thought I'd offer interviews in the UK and Berlin, if that's OK. It's important that Jürgen Müller's involved. As the general manager, he and the personnel officer will need to work together closely on the future recruitment campaign in Berlin.

Jackie Yes, good idea. Well, David, I can see you've got it all under control. Just keep me posted, please.

David No problem.

Jackie Oh, sorry, I've got to run. I have a meeting about disciplinary procedures in about five minutes. Oh, and by the way, I'll be back in the office again on Thursday, so perhaps we can talk again then.

Say whether the following statements about the text are true (✔), false (✗) or you don't know (?). Correct the false statements.

1 Jürgen Müller is general manager of the Berlin office. ☐
2 The personnel officer they are looking for must have 2–5 years' specialist experience. ☐
3 Applicants should have either a qualification in human resources management or a university degree. ☐
4 Jackie is responsible for the recruitment of the personnel officer in Berlin. ☐
5 David is offering people interviews in the UK and in Berlin. ☐
6 They are looking for a personnel officer because of a recent merger. ☐
7 Jackie will conduct the interviews. ☐

11   Find a word or phrase in the dialogue which means the following:

1 to discuss something
2 (have been) given official approval
3 the opposite of 'specialist'
4 inside a company
5 when two companies become one
6 newspaper or magazine for a specific profession
7 to keep somebody informed
8 ways of warning employees officially that they are breaking the rules

12   Word families: Complete the following sentences with words related to the key words – 'employ' and 'recruit'. (You might need to add prefixes or suffixes and change the form.) Here's some help with 'employ' to get you started.

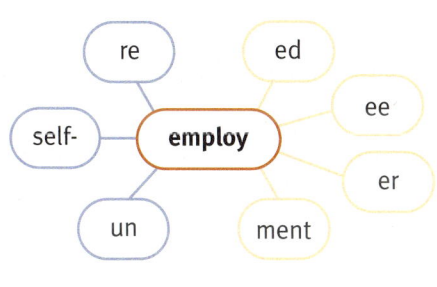

employ

1 We are unable to use people who are *self-employed* unless they work for several different companies.
2 There are more people on the job markets when levels of _____ are high.
3 She told her _____ she was looking for another job.
4 We engaged six new _____ in the last quarter.
5 We _____ her in the same position when she returned from maternity leave.

recruit

6 Last year we _____ two team leaders for our call centre.
7 We've revised our overall _____ procedure because of the new employment legislation.

13 **Match the definitions (a–g) with the different sources of recruitment (1–7). Which sources does your company use to find new employees? Which sources do you think are most effective?**

1	word of mouth	a	Internet recruitment sites for job seekers
2	internal advertising	b	magazines for specific professions
3	media advertising	c	organizations that match jobs with people's experience
4	advertising in trade press	d	letters received from people looking for a job (but not responding to an advertisement)
5	online recruitment	e	advertising vacancies inside a company
6	recruitment agencies	f	advertising jobs in the local or national press
7	unsolicited applications	g	passing on information by networking or talking to people

14 **First study the useful phrases for exchanging information, making suggestions and agreeing and disagreeing. Then look at your profile in the partner files and role-play the situation with your partner.**

PARTNER FILES Partner A File 01, p. 60 Partner B File 01, p. 62

USEFUL PHRASES

Exchanging information
Can we just have a word about …?
I'd like to be up to date on what's happening.
So where/what are you planning to …?
Well, firstly I thought I would …
I'll look into it (though).

Making suggestions
I suggest we …
In my opinion …
What do you think about …?
Actually, there is someone in the company who …
Well, we should consider …

Agreeing and disagreeing
I agree./I disagree.
I think so too.
You have got a point (there).
Yes, (that's a) good idea.
(I'm) Not sure I agree with you there.

Read the article on the benefits of using recruitment advertising agencies and discuss the questions below.

The benefits of using recruitment advertising agencies

Traditionally, recruitment advertising agencies are responsible for designing, writing and placing job advertisements in the media. While this is still their main responsibility, they are now offering companies other services such as internal employee communication and the development of company literature, websites and corporate identity (CI) in general. This change in focus reflects changes in the world of business. More and more companies now recognize the value of good employees and just how important it is to hold on to and attract skilled staff. Effective communication can help build bridges between the staff and the employer and provide both with an identity they can be proud of.

Here are just some of the benefits of using recruitment advertising agencies:

- Agencies have the expertise that companies do not always have in-house. This includes not only the ability to write and design ads but also the knowledge of, and relationships with, the press and media. Agencies can negotiate better prices and know which type of advert – whether in a newspaper, trade magazine or online – can best reach the candidates you are looking for.
- Many larger agencies operate in wide, even global, markets and represent companies of different sizes across many different sectors or industries. This can help them understand a company's position within the recruitment marketplace and to see an employer's greatest selling points.
- Developing a new recruitment campaign or a new corporate identity requires a lot of time and money. Using an agency to handle this for you allows you to concentrate on running your company. By making one agency responsible for all your recruitment needs, you can make sure your company has a consistent message and thus attracts the right staff to fit your corporate culture and share your company's goals.

OVER TO YOU

Does your company use recruitment advertising agencies for designing and placing job advertisements? What are the advantages and disadvantages in your field of business?

How does your company deal with corporate identity? Is the same agency – or department in your company – responsible for both functions?

2 Selection

Work with a partner. Decide whether you agree or disagree with these statements about job applications and interviews.

	Agree	Disagree
1 A curriculum vitae should be no longer than two A4 pages.	☐	☐
2 It is good practice to include a photograph on a curriculum vitae.	☐	☐
3 It is not necessary for applicants to put their date of birth on their application.	☐	☐
4 References which candidates supply with their applications could be false so you shouldn't always believe them.	☐	☐
5 You should enclose copies of certificates and exam results with a job application.	☐	☐
6 It is a good idea to supply applicants with a job description and person specification *before* the interview.	☐	☐
7 Applicants should never wear jeans to an interview.	☐	☐
8 At an interview it is appropriate to ask female applicants about their plans for starting a family.	☐	☐

DID YOU KNOW?

In the US a *Lebenslauf* is called a 'resumé' (also spelled 'resume' or 'résumé').
In the UK it is called a 'curriculum vitae' or 'CV'.
A 'reference' is a letter written by someone who knows the applicant (usually the current or a former employer) and can give information about the applicant's abilities. The person who supplies a reference is called a 'referee' (UK).

1 Look at the online job advertisement for Virgin Atlantic on page 15. Is it similar to a job advert from your company? If so, how? What do you think would attract applicants to apply for this job?

2 Match these phrases from the Virgin Atlantic advert (1–8) to the definitions on the right (a–h).

1 to create rapport
2 to understand their needs
3 to provide advice
4 to promote a range of services
5 to attend an interview
6 to be notified of the outcome
7 to receive a shift allowance
8 to be entitled to a benefits package

a to have the right to extra advantages on top of salary
b to get extra money for working 'unsociable' hours
c to suggest the best way to do something
d to visit a company to discuss a job
e to develop a good relationship
f to be told the results of a decision
g to attract people's attention to what you offer
h to know what they want

Travel Adviser – The Office, Crawley

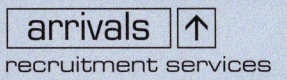

The Image

At Virgin Atlantic we're renowned for our high standards of customer service and know that first impressions count.

Our Reservations Team creates a rapport with our callers, understanding their needs and providing advice and assistance on all their travel requirements. The responsibilities are varied and include promoting Virgin's ever expanding range of services, whilst maintaining our high levels of customer service.

The Demands

Speaking to around 100 callers each day, you need to be self-motivated whilst maintaining high levels of accuracy in this busy environment. On your shift pattern there will be a variety of start and finish times including some early mornings and late nights. Don't forget, shift work means you might have to work weekends and bank holidays.

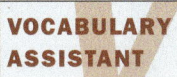

The Interview

The interview process consists of a group interview, which will last approximately one and a half hours. You will then take part in a series of exercises. Our experienced recruitment assessors will monitor your performance and look for specific competencies such as customer relationships, service orientation and attention to detail. If you are successful through the group stage, you will be asked to attend an individual interview with two recruitment assessors. You will be notified of the outcome of this final stage in writing.

The Rewards

The starting salary is generous and, as a shift worker, you will also receive a shift allowance. There is an increase to the basic salary on successful completion of your six-month probationary period.

On completion of the probationary period, you will be entitled to a generous holiday allowance and a discretionary benefits package which includes a pension, life assurance, Virgin Group discount scheme and concessionary travel (one of the best in the business!).

VOCABULARY ASSISTANT

competencies *Kompetenzen, Fähigkeiten*   concessionary *ermäßigt*
discretionary *nach Ermessen*   probationary period *Probezeit*
renowned *renommiert*   shift allowance *Schichtzuschlag*

3   Some applicants had questions about the job. Supply the answers.

1   "What are the hours of work exactly?"
2   "What are the main responsibilities of the job?"
3   "How many calls will I have to handle a day?"
4   "Where is the job located?"
5   "What will the interview consist of and how will we learn the results?"
6   "Are there any other payments in addition to the basic salary?"
7   "What other benefits do you offer?"
8   "Does everyone receive the same benefits package?"

4   **What details would you expect to find in a curriculum vitae? Complete the mind map with items from the box. Can you add any more items to the mind map?**

a brief summary of your work experience and abilities • dates of previous employment • duties in previous jobs • relevant courses attended • full contact details • language skills • main exams or degree • marital status • name and address • achievements/skills in career • outstanding qualities • previous employers • nationality • professional qualification or title • school and university details • qualifications or certificates from on-the-job training • specializations/publications

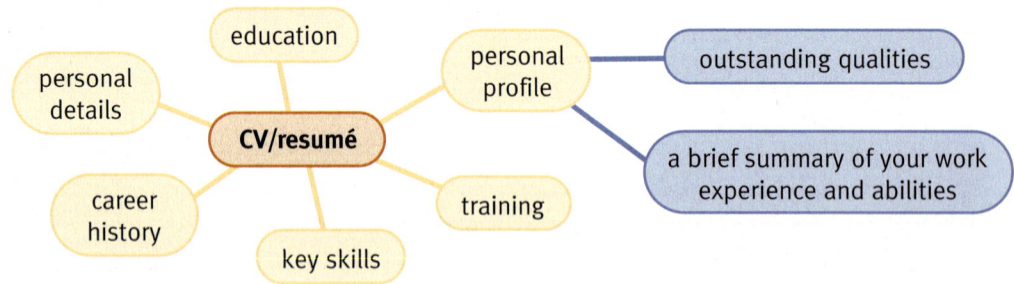

Now put these main headings into a logical order in which they might appear on a CV.

☐ education   ☐ personal profile   ☐ career history

☐ key skills   ☐ training   ☐ personal details

5   **Read the letter on page 17 and label it with the following items (a–j).**

a   invitation to an interview
b   acknowledgement of the applicant's letter
c   polite ending
d   subject of the letter
e   contact details for arranging an interview
f   salutation
g   letterhead
h   note that something has been sent with the letter
i   complimentary close
j   procedure if invited to a second interview

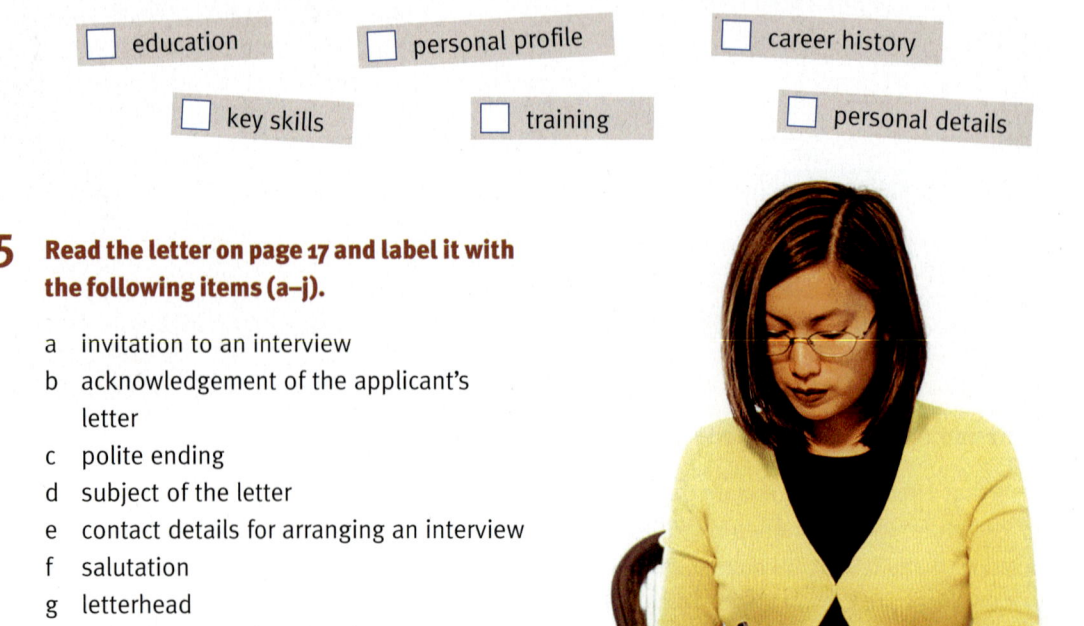

□1   **Mobile plus GmbH**

Bachstr. 244 • 12569 Berlin

Ms Melanie Smith   25 August 20..
Flat 4
21 Lymington Road
Epsom, Surrey
EP5 3RE
UK
            □2

Dear Ms Smith

            □3

Application for Call Centre Team Leader   □4

Thank you for your letter of 15 August and your curriculum vitae, applying for a
Team Leader position in our call centre in London.   □5

We currently have two vacancies for Team Leaders in our UK call centre and we would like to
invite you for an initial interview at our London office in the next two weeks. If successful, you will
then be asked to attend a full day assessment centre with seven other applicants next month, after
which a final decision will be made.

□6   We will pay your travelling expenses to the interview and to the assessment centre, if selected.
During the assessment centre, which will last from 9 am–5 pm, lunch with the other applicants and
assessors is provided as part of the day. If you need overnight accommodation, then you will be
booked into a local hotel near our office. Full details of the assessment centre procedure will be sent
to you in advance if you are selected.

□7   We would be grateful if you could telephone Jenny Mills, Personnel Assistant, in London on (0044)
020 845 9554 ext 2317 to arrange a convenient time for the interview. Please find enclosed an
application form which we would like you to complete and take along to the interview with you.

We wish you success at the interview and look forward to welcoming you to our London office.
            □8

Yours sincerely   □9

Daniela Guth
Recruitment Officer

enc   □10

6   True or false? Correct the false statements.

1   Melanie has applied for a position as Call Centre Assistant.
2   She sent a CV with her letter of application.
3   The whole recruitment process will be completed within two weeks.
4   The company will pay for Melanie's journey to the interview.
5   Applicants will be told what the assessment centre procedure involves when they get to the
    company.
6   They want Melanie to complete an application form.
7   Melanie has to call Berlin to arrange the interview.

7 **Put the following parts of a letter into the correct order. Then check your answer with the model letter on page 74.**

a We would like to invite you to attend an interview at this office and would be grateful if you could telephone the undersigned as soon as possible to arrange a suitable date and time.

b We look forward to welcoming you to our offices.

c Thank you for your letter of 2 September, applying for the position of … with this company.

d If you have any questions, please raise them when you call to arrange the interview.

f Enclosed is a copy of the person specification and job description for this job, which we would like you to familiarize yourself with before the interview.

e Alternatively, you can go to our website for these documents and other information about the company. A map showing the location of our office is also enclosed.

DID YOU KNOW?

Remember: when you write business letters the general 'rule' is …

- when you don't know the person's name:
  Dear Sir or Madam
  Yours faithfully

- when you know the person's name:
  Dear Ms/Mrs/Mr Brownley
  Yours sincerely

- when you know the person well:
  Dear James
  Best regards/Best wishes/Yours/ Kind regards/Sincerely

8 **First study the useful phrases below for arranging an appointment. Then look at your profile in the partner files and, as a follow-up to the letter on page 17, make a telephone call to arrange an interview.**

PARTNER FILES ➤ Partner A File 02, p. 60
Partner B File 02, p. 62

Tomorrow's bad for me, I'm afraid.

USEFUL PHRASES

Arranging an appointment
What date would be convenient for you?
What time would suit you?
Would Monday at 10.30 suit you?
Is the 5th of March at 6 pm convenient?
How about 10 am?
Tuesday the 8th of July would be good for me.
Monday's bad for me, I'm afraid.
That sounds fine.
Yes, that would be good for me.
I think that should be possible.

When a company employs new staff, they are 'taken on' (UK) or 'hired' (US). When these employees then decide to leave, they 'resign' or 'hand in their notice/resignation'.

When employees have to leave because they did something wrong, they 'are dismissed' or their contracts are 'terminated'. (More informally, they are 'sacked' (UK) or 'fired' (US).) If they have to leave because a company can no longer employ them (eg due to bankruptcy or downsizing), the employee is 'made redundant' (UK), 'let go' (US) or even 'offered early retirement'.

When an employee is 'laid off' (to 'lay off'), it is usually only temporary (for a season or because of a drop in production) but sometimes it can be permanent.

9 **Complete the sentences with expressions from above.**

1 My best marketing assistant _____ . She's got herself another job with more money!

2 Will we be able to _____ a replacement when John hands in his _____ ?

3 We can't continue working in these freezing temperatures, so we'll have to _____ six workers until the end of February.

4 Those staff who can't relocate to the new factory in the north when we close down will be _____ .

5 Fill me in on the details; I believe one of our shop assistants has been _____ for stealing, is that right?

6 A new directive from head office has been introduced that all employees over 63 will be _____ .

10 **Sort the following interview strategies into a logical order.**

☐ a Establish rapport and relax the candidate.

☐ b Read the candidate's application and have it with you at the interview.

☐ c Use open questions as much as possible to ensure the candidate gives detailed answers.

☐ d Allow the candidate to do most of the talking but keep the interview focussed.

☐ e Before finishing the interview, explain what will happen next and by when.

☐ f Use a quiet office away from noise and interruptions.

☐ g Welcome the applicant warmly, introduce yourself and explain the structure of the interview.

☐ h Allow the candidate time for his or her own questions.

Can you add any other tips? What cultural differences do you think would influence such a list?

11   **Look at these extracts from Jenny's interview with Melanie Smith. What kind of questions does Jenny ask? What kind of answers do they require?**

Jenny   ... I think that fills you in on the requirements of the job. So, could you tell me about your experience as a team leader in your present job?

Melanie   Yes, I've been with my present company for five years. I started as a member of the call centre and was promoted to a team leader two years ago. I'm one of eight team leaders and we cover two shifts, seven days a week.

Jenny   Could you explain what that involves?

Melanie   Yes, I'm responsible for ten call centre operators and I report to the call centre supervisor. As you can see from my CV, I also did customer service in a production company for six years before that.

* * *

Jenny   Could you outline some of the problems you've had to deal with since you became a team leader?

Melanie   Well, they relate mainly to difficult customers and to one or two negative relationships in the group.

Jenny   Could you enlarge on that?

Melanie   As far as staff relationships are concerned, if the problem is not solved by discussion and liaison within the team, then we can usually move people to another team. The team leaders meet weekly to discuss the overall situation and we operate a very flexible call centre where the staff can move around different sections to gain more experience.

Jenny   And how do you go about dealing with difficult customers or with customers who have a complaint?

Melanie   We have a directive that says that a customer who is not happy about something should be transferred to a team leader immediately. It's one of our specific responsibilities.

Otherwise my staff are instructed to tell the customer that I will call them back as soon as possible. If I'm not there, then another team leader deals with it.

* * *

Jenny   What aspect of your job do you like best, Melanie?

Melanie   I particularly enjoy dealing with customers. I think I have an ability to build a good rapport with people on the telephone – this is why I went into this type of work – and I believe I am good at it.

* * *

Jenny   Why do you want to leave your present job?

Melanie   Part of the call centre is being transferred to another location in the South. My partner has a good job in this area and we have two children at school. I don't really want to move at this time, although my company did ask me if I would like to relocate.

Jenny   I see. Thank you. As you know, the next part of the interview process would be an assessment centre ...

12   **What do these words and expressions from the dialogue mean? Tick the correct definition.**

1   to fill someone in
☐ a   to complete a form
☐ b   to give more information so they have all the details

2   to be promoted
☐ a   to move to a higher position in a company
☐ b   to take a lower position in a company

3   to outline something
☐ a   to summarize
☐ b   to give a detailed explanation

4   liaison within the team
☐ a   exchange of information between team members
☐ b   a romantic relationship

5   to complain
☐ a   to say everything is fine
☐ b   to say that you are unhappy about something

6   directive
☐ a   a rule
☐ b   a special person who deals with something

7   to relocate
☐ a   to move to a new area (with your job)
☐ b   to be asked to leave your job

13   **Use the following form to make notes about the interview. Do you think Melanie should be short-listed for the assessment centre? Complete gap 10 below with your own ideas.**

Interview notes

Name of applicant: (1) _Melanie Smith_

Job applied for: (2) _____

Date of interview: 04 September

Experience

a   5 years' experience in a similar position.

b   (3) _____

c   (4) _____

Level of responsibility

a   reports directly to call centre supervisor

b   (5) _____

c   (6) _____

Specific abilities

Staff relationships: (7) _____
_____

Customer service: good communication skills,
(8) _____
_____

Reason for leaving (9) _____
_____

Suitability for the position

Melanie appears to have the right qualifications and experience to undertake this position. Her communication skills and relationship with staff (10) _____
_____
_____

Recommendation for shortlist to assessment centre: Yes ☐   No ☐

The language of interview questioning
Look at the type of questions the interviewer asks in the dialogue on page 20. These are known as 'open questions' and usually avoid 'yes' and 'no' answers. Below are some examples of the way you can word your interview questions to get people talking about themselves and their experience.

What …?
What aspect of your job do you like best?
What do you know about …?
What experience have you had of …?

How …?
How do you go about dealing with …?
How would you handle …?

Why …?
Why do you want to leave your present job?
Why did you deal with the situation in that way?

OR
I'd like you to tell me …
Could you give me an example of …?
Interesting. What else do you …?

14 **Change these 'closed' questions, which could be answered with 'yes' or 'no', to open ones.**

1   Do you get on well with your present supervisor?
2   Have you had many staff problems to deal with in your current job?
3   Do you consider yourself good at customer service?
4   Are you used to working shifts?
5   Are you able to work on your own initiative?
6   Do you work well under pressure?

15 **First make a list of questions you would ask at an interview for your own job.**
Then exchange your list with a partner and practise asking and answering the questions
in an interview situation. Try to use the phrases in the box for establishing rapport
and asking follow-up questions.

Establishing rapport and relaxing the candidate
It's nice to welcome you here and I hope you'll enjoy the
   interview.
Please feel free to ask any questions you may have.
I'm going to start by … and then we'll talk about …. Finally,
   we can deal with any points you would like to raise.

Asking follow-up questions
Could you tell me some more about …?
What exactly do you mean by …?
Could you enlarge on that?

16 **Word families: Complete the following sentences with words related to the key words.**
(You might need to add prefixes or suffixes and change the form.)

apply   1   There were two _____ who were far better than the others in terms of
previous experience.

2   All candidates must complete an _____ form to bring to the interview.

3   The employment legislation is not _____ to people working less than
25 hours per week.

select   4   As we had a lot of candidates for the advertised position, we were able to be very

           _____ .

      5   We offer a _____ of benefits to our personnel in addition to salary.

assess   6   In some types of recruitment, _____ centres are used regularly.

      7   It was difficult to _____ the final two shortlisted applicants as they had such mixed skills.

Exactly how important is age in the selection of candidates?
Read the comments below and say which opinion(s) you agree with.

1 It is not relevant to ask someone's age. You can work it out roughly from their CV and, anyway, the important thing is whether or not they have the ability to do the job, not how old they are.

3 I'm afraid I can't agree with you on that. Older people are not as flexible, they expect higher salaries and they get sick a lot. And they have trouble fitting into a young team. Companies want younger employees who can bring in fresh ideas and are not so expensive!

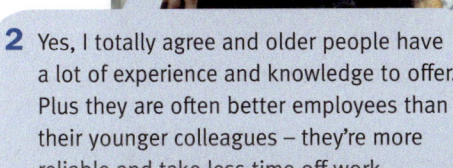

2 Yes, I totally agree and older people have a lot of experience and knowledge to offer. Plus they are often better employees than their younger colleagues – they're more reliable and take less time off work.

4 You can't run a company efficiently with young, inexperienced people. You need to retain older managers to train the younger ones and you have to organize effective succession planning in a company. There should be capacity for a broad age range and diverse experience in all areas of the business.

5 I think laws on age discrimination are wrong. Why should the government be able to tell us who to hire? Only the companies know which people are right – or wrong – for the job. The government shouldn't tell us how to run our business.

OVER TO YOU

How would you feel if, after 20 years in your profession, you were considered too old for the job?
Do you think legislation on age discrimination will help the situation?
What kind of policies does your company have on age discrimination?

3 Employee relations

CLOCK-IN

Here are some word partnerships that apply to employee relations. Some of the letters are missing. Complete the words and then match them with the definitions on the right.

s☐☐ dis☐☐☐m☐☐☐t☐☐n ¹

con☐☐☐ct of em☐☐☐☐m☐☐t ²

☐qu☐☐ pay ³

mat☐r☐☐☐y l☐☐ve ⁴

workp☐☐☐☐ inj☐☐☐es ⁵

s☐ort-t☐m☐ w☐rk☐☐g ⁶

disc☐pl☐n☐☐y and gr☐☐van☐e procedure ⁷

w☐☐k-re☐☐ted st☐ess ⁸

a reduced working hours, usually when a company has a decrease in production
b accidents that happen at work
c to treat someone of either sex unfairly
d period of absence for a woman who has had a baby
e the same salary for men and women
f stress caused by negative factors in the job
g procedure when an employee breaks the rules and what the employee can do if unhappy with a decision
h written details given to an employee to confirm terms and conditions

1 A recruitment officer, June Stewart, and a team leader, Mario Rossi, are discussing terms and conditions with Karin Grau, who has just been offered a position with Business Systems Ltd at their Manchester office. Read this extract from the second interview and discuss whether the interview procedure is different from the way things are done in your company.

June We'd like to tell you something about conditions of employment. Of course, they'll also be described in the contract of employment and the company handbook, as well as in the offer letter.

Mario Some employment procedures are different from those in Germany, Karin, but there is generally more flexibility here, I think. Please ask about anything you are not sure of.

June So, let's start with your hours. Normal working hours are 9–6 Monday to Friday, with an hour for lunch. We currently operate a 40-hour week (plus lunches). I'm afraid we don't operate flexitime yet and there may be overtime during busy periods. This is either paid or given as time off in lieu.

Karin I see.

Mario By the way, we're currently looking at more flexible working arrangements for our employees, but that's still in the future.

Karin OK. Could you tell me what happens if I am ill?

June We pay you for the first 12 weeks of sickness and operate a company 'Permanent Health Insurance' scheme which continues to pay you after that.

Mario   If you're ill, Karin, we expect you to phone in as early as possible on the first day to tell us and then to keep us informed after that.

Karin   Yes, that's clear. Could you tell me something about the holiday allowance?

June   Your annual paid holiday is 20 days, rising to 25 after two years' service. You must clear dates first with your department head, of course.

Karin   I have a week's holiday booked in two months' time – will you honour this?

Mario   I'm sure that won't be a problem as it's only a week. We can discuss it in detail later.

Karin   Great. Would it be possible to see the contract?

June   Yes, of course. One will be sent with the offer letter.

Mario   We'll be taking up references with your previous and present employer. I know in Germany you would normally include references with your application, but as you know, here in the UK we prefer to apply for references ourselves. Which is why we'll make the offer of employment 'subject to satisfactory reference'.

Karin   Yes, I understand. I've given details of my referees on the application form. My present employer in Hamburg knows I'm leaving, so you can go ahead and contact them. I'll tell them to expect a letter from you.

Mario   Well thanks, Karin. I hope you'll be joining us soon and look forward to welcoming you to the department. Maybe you'd like to meet some of the team over a bite of lunch? We'll all be going to the canteen in around 15 minutes.

Karin   That sounds nice, thanks.

June   Yes, well, I'll leave you to look after Karin. We'll get the offer letter, contract and handbook in the post within the next 24 hours. Could you please let us know if you want to accept the job offer by the beginning of next week?

Karin   Yes, of course.

June   Once you sign and return a copy of the contract, we can apply for references. The sooner, the better, right?

Karin   Right. Thank you both very much. I feel very positive about everything.

True or false? Correct the false statements.

1   Karin will be working flexitime in her new job.
2   She will be paid for the first 12 weeks if she is ill.
3   Her holiday entitlement is 20 days from the date she starts with Business Systems.
4   She sent in copies of her references with her application.
5   She hasn't told her employer in Hamburg that she's leaving yet.
6   She will receive the offer letter in two weeks.

DID YOU KNOW?

The practice whereby employees can choose exactly what time they start and finish work is called 'flexible working', 'flexible hours', 'flextime' (US) and 'flexitime' (UK).

2 **Complete the puzzle with words from the dialogue.**

Across

6 the opposite of temporary
7 ways of doing things
8 instead (of sth else)
9 to get official permission:
  to ... sth with sb

Down

1 people who supply the information
  in 4 down
2 to agree to sth, to keep a promise
3 an official written agreement
4 letter containing all terms and
  conditions: ... letter
5 information about how well you
  worked in your previous job(s)

3 **Complete the table with words and phrases from the box.**

Working time	Employment status	Absence	Ending employment
shift work	trial period	annual leave	

shift work • notice period • annual leave • part-time employment • trial period •
core time • sick leave • public holiday • resignation • vacation • dismissal •
fixed-term contract • six-day week • redundancy • temporary employment • flexitime •
probationary period • holiday entitlement

Compare your table with a partner's and try to add words to each category.

4 **Word families: Complete the following sentences with words related to the key word 'flex'.
(You might need to add prefixes or suffixes and change the form.)**

1 We have a very _____ system in the company for our staff who need time off
  work for childcare.

2 We've been operating _____ in the company since the early 90s.

3 There is little or no _____ for our staff in terms of hours of work as they have

  to be around when our customers need them.

4 Unfortunately, our managing director is very _____ when it comes to deadlines.

5 **Look at the list of points that should be mentioned in a contract of employment in the UK. Match them to the extracts from some model contracts (a–j).**

1 date the employment begins
2 rate of pay and when/how paid
3 normal hours of work/overtime/shift patterns
4 holiday entitlement (including public holidays)
5 job title (or a brief description of the job)

6 location of workplace
7 notice period
8 sick pay provision
9 pension scheme terms
10 disciplinary rules and grievance procedure

a The amount of notice you are required to give or be given by your employer in the first four years is four weeks.

b A copy of the company's disciplinary procedure is attached to this contract and employees are asked to read it carefully.

c Your basic salary will be £35,000 per annum, payable monthly in arrears by credit transfer to your bank or building society.

d Your normal place of work will be the above address. From time to time the company may require you to work at other sites on a temporary basis.

e Your employment begins on 1 January 20…

f The company does not offer a pension scheme but provides access to a stakeholder pension. Details can be obtained from the personnel department.

g You may be required to work on a public holiday. If so, you are entitled to time off in lieu.

h Normal hours of work are $37\frac{1}{2}$ per week, 9 am to 5.30 pm Monday to Friday, with one unpaid hour for lunch each day.

i You must inform the office by 10 am on the first day of absence. Failure to do so may render you subject to disciplinary action and may also bar you from sick pay.

j Your current job title and responsibilities are detailed in Schedule 1 and may be amended from time to time. Any changes will be discussed with you fully and notified to you in writing.

VOCABULARY ASSISTANT to amend *(ab)ändern* to bar sb from sth *jdn von etwas ausschließen* to be entitled to sth *Anspruch auf etw haben* disciplinary action *Disziplinarverfahren* grievance *Beschwerde* in arrears *rückwirkend* to render *zur Folge haben*

How are contracts similar or different in your country? What points must be mentioned?

BEST PRACTICE

The language of contracts
The language used in contracts of employment is highly formal and includes fixed phrases, formal vocabulary and the passive and the *will* future. Some examples are given below.

Fixed phrases
will be notified in writing
payable monthly in arrears
failure to do so
subject to disciplinary action

Use of formal vocabulary

to render		to make
to amend	*instead of*	to change
to be entitled to		to have the right to
to notify		to tell

Use of passive
employees **are asked** …
you **may be required** …
details **can be obtained** …
more information **can be found** in …
employees **are expected** …

Use of future
your place of work **will be** …
any changes **will be discussed** …

6 **Complete these sentences with words and phrases from the box.**

> can be found • notified in writing • are expected • may be required •
> notify • payable monthly in arrears • will be discussed • are asked •
> subject to disciplinary action • are entitled to

1 Full details of the sick pay scheme _____ in the staff handbook.

2 You _____ to work in another office of the company from time to time.

3 Employees _____ to work overtime as and when needed.

4 Changes to your contract _____ and you'll be _____

_____ .

5 You _____ four weeks' holiday per annum after completion of six

months' probation.

6 Your salary is _____ on the last day of each month.

7 Employees _____ to _____ the company of

any absence by 10 am on the first day.

8 You may be _____ if you fail to do this.

7 **An offer letter and a rejection letter have been mixed up. Look at the paragraphs a–j on the opposite page, sort them and put them into the correct order.**

Offer letter

d – c –

Rejection letter

g – b –

a   We would like you to start on 1 November 20.., if possible. During your first week you will participate in an induction seminar to familiarize you fully with the company. Full details of this will be sent to you nearer the time.

b   Thank you for attending the interview for the above position. It was very nice meeting you.

c   Further to your recent interviews, we have pleasure in offering you the position of International Marketing Assistant in the UK Marketing Department, based at this address, at a commencing salary of £29,000 per annum. This offer is conditional on receiving satisfactory references from your present and last employers and to the satisfactory completion of a three-month probationary period on either side.

d   Dear Ms Grau

e   We appreciate your interest and would like to take this opportunity to wish you every success in your future career.

f   Please let us know as soon as possible if you would like to accept by signing and returning one copy of the contract. We will then take up references. We hope you will join us and very much look forward to hearing from you.

g   Dear Mr Chevalier

h   We have now fully considered your application and regret we are unable to offer you a second interview on this occasion.

i   Basic hours of work are normally 9 am to 6 pm Monday to Friday, including an hour for lunch. It will be necessary for you to work overtime as and when required. Holiday entitlement is 20 days per annum, rising to 25 after two years' service. Normally holiday cannot be taken during the probationary period. All terms, conditions and benefits are detailed in the handbook and contract enclosed.

j   We will hold your details pending and let you know if a suitable opening occurs in the future.

8   Look at these words and phrases from the letters above, and match the words in italics with a–h.

1	a *commencing* salary of …	a	enclosed
2	the offer is *conditional on* receiving …	b	learn about
3	*probationary* period	c	starting
4	*accompanying* details	d	year
5	per *annum*	e	subject to
6	are *detailed* in …	f	set out
7	to *familiarize*	g	until we have something available
8	We will hold your details *pending* …	h	trial

9 Work with a partner to role-play a discussion about terms and conditions of employment. Partner A is the personnel officer and Partner B is the interviewee. Use some of the phrases below.

PARTNER FILES   Partner A   File 03, p. 60
    Partner B   File 03, p. 62

USEFUL PHRASES

Giving information
I'd like to tell you something about …
Please ask about anything you are not sure of.
I'm sure that's not a problem …
I'm afraid we don't …

Requesting information
Could you tell me … ?
Will you honour this?
Would it be possible to … ?
Could you please let us know … ?

10 Read this article from an HR trade magazine and complete the gaps with words from the list.

behaviour • breaking • conditions • disciplinary • entitled •
entitlement • occur • policy • representative • safety

Dealing with grievances

Problems can _____ [1] in the best run companies for many reasons, such as over terms and _____ [2], management decisions, discrimination (on grounds of race, sex, disability and religion), sexual harassment, bullying, health and _____ [3] issues.

Within two months of starting a job, employees are _____ [4] to a written statement setting down the main conditions of their employment. As well as information on pay, hours, holiday _____ [5] and notice periods, the statement must also cover what the company will do if they have to discipline an employee for _____ [6] the rules (the warning procedure) and who the employee can apply to if they are dissatisfied with a _____ [7] decision. All employees have the right to be accompanied by another employee or a union _____ [8] (if applicable) at any disciplinary interview.

A disciplinary procedure would normally be used when an employee does not follow company _____ [9], breaks rules or displays inappropriate workplace behaviour. Employees must be fully informed of their inappropriate _____ [10] and given an opportunity to explain themselves. The procedure should be handled in a private and respectful manner and the employee's previous record should be taken into account.

VOCABULARY ASSISTANT
to accompany *begleiten*   bullying
Mobbing   disability *Behinderung*
harassment *Belästigung*
to take into account *berücksichtigen*

DID YOU KNOW?

The word 'mobbing' is not used in English. Instead English speakers use the words 'harassment' or 'bullying'. Other words are 'victimization' and 'intimidation'.

Now discuss the article and the following questions.

1 What should employees in your company do if they have a grievance? What role, if any, does the works council *(Betriebsrat)* play?
2 What are some of the problems that can lead to disciplinary procedures?
3 How do you discipline staff if they do something wrong?

11 **Below are some headlines from articles on HR issues. In pairs decide what you think they refer to and then discuss your answers with the whole group.**

1 **Absence levels rising ...**

2 **Is there a doctor in the house?**

3 **Women sue over sex discrimination**

4 Deaths from overwork (Karoshi) increase in Japan

5 **Staff quit over Internet use and abuse**

6 **Wellness management – a growing necessity?**

7 **US ban on smoking in the workplace reduces heart attacks**

8 **Consultation on workplace noise rules**

Have any of these issues arisen in your company? How did you deal with them?

12 **Number the following workplace stress factors in order of importance (1 most stressful, 10 least stressful). Compare your results with a partner's.**

- [ ] interpersonal relationships at work (problems with co-workers)
- [ ] tight deadlines (pressure to get work done in time)
- [ ] intimidation from supervisors
- [ ] work environment/equipment (unsatisfactory working conditions)
- [ ] workload
- [ ] job security (fear of losing one's job)
- [ ] working hours
- [ ] low autonomy (working under constant supervision)
- [ ] repetitive work
- [ ] work/life balance (finding time for responsibilities at home)

What health and safety measures is your company taking to reduce stress levels in staff?

13   **Which of the health and safety measures below do you think are typical of a) factories b) offices or shops or c) any environment? Work with a partner to add items to the list.**

1   carry out fire drills $\boxed{c}$
2   make sure furniture is properly adjusted   ☐
3   prevent exposure to harmful substances   ☐
4   provide eye tests   ☐
5   post safety signs   ☐

6   remove dangerous obstacles   ☐
7   provide safety equipment (hard hats, etc)   ☐
8   do risk assessments   ☐
9   train first aiders   ☐
10   wear protective clothing   ☐

Which measures have been introduced at your workplace?

CLOCK-OUT

What do the figures represent in the following article about workplace injuries? Read the article to find out, then discuss the questions which follow.

a   7.5 million   b   249   c   127,000   d   563,000

Workplace injuries

- A factory worker had his right leg amputated below the knee when he was run over by a fork lift truck.
- A team manager tripped on some carpeting and fell down the stairs at work, breaking her ankle. She was unable to walk for several months and is still in pain and using a stick almost a year later. She has been unable to return to work since.
- A nurse has been off work for six months with severe back pain resulting from lifting patients. She is unable to drive or sit down for long periods and is awaiting an operation.

According to a 2003 report by the Health and Safety Executive, a British government agency responsible for health and safety issues at work, over 7.5 million working days are lost each year in the UK due to accidents at the workplace. The report went on to say that the amount of time and money lost because of employee injury is probably actually much higher, as the law requires that only fatal (ie those resulting in death) and serious injuries are reported.

Figures for 2001 and 2002 indicate that while only 249 people died in accidents at work (a decrease of 15% from previous years), there were 27,477 non-fatal major injuries, including amputations, eye injuries and broken arms and legs, and over 127,000 injuries, which were less serious but still kept the employees out of work for over three days. Two of the main causes of non-fatal injuries are slipping and tripping up (37% of the total).

While there is a growing awareness among employers about the prevention of serious accidents at work, the greatest workplace health problem today is back pain and strain to the neck, arm and hands. Lifting loads that are too heavy, sitting incorrectly and doing repetitive work for long periods of time are typical causes of such injuries. Finally, a rapidly growing area of ill health relates to mental health problems such as stress and anxiety, of which there were 563,000 sufferers in the UK last year. In fact, work-related stress has doubled over the past ten years and is becoming one of the major problems facing companies and HR professionals today.

OVER TO YOU

How do you think these figures relate to statistics from your country?
What procedure do you have in your company for reporting workplace accidents and injuries?
What training or assistance do you offer employees to prevent back pain in their daily work?

4 HR development

CLOCK-IN

Discuss the statements below with a partner. Do you agree or disagree with them?
Are they key HR concepts? What aspects of HR development do you think the statements refer to?

1 "Nobody can guarantee lifetime employment, but there's a lot you can do to improve the odds."
2 "Quality feedback improves performance."
3 "Those most at risk of leaving are new employees."
4 "All animals are equal, but some are more equal than others."

1 Match the HR development practices in the box with their definitions (1–8) below.

> appraisal • equal opportunity policies • flexible working practices •
> induction programme • long-term individual development • mentoring •
> secondment • team development

1 _flexible working practices_____: to adapt the way of working (flexitime, teleworking, etc) to suit the diverse needs of employees' lives

2 _____: the temporary transfer of an employee to another organization or part of the company

3 _____: continually updating and promoting the professional development of employees

4 _____: regular evaluation of an employee's performance, development requirements and potential

5 _____: to maintain fair working practices and equal treatment for each employee

6 _____: to motivate a group of employees to work together effectively

7 _____: to provide an employee with an experienced person who can assist with professional development and offer support and advice

8 _____: to inform new staff about the company and its procedures and to help them to settle successfully into their new job

Which aspects of development mentioned above does your company use? Which do you think are most effective?

2 Work with a partner. Match the staff problems (1–4) with the best solution (a–d). Would you recommend a different form of HR development in any of the examples?

Natasha

1 *Shop floor team leader: You know, I only started here four months ago but I'm already thinking about leaving. Gerry, the shop floor supervisor, is always correcting me, always telling me that things are done differently here and he's so negative. He never gives me any real help. And my team is also against me. I just don't know how much longer I can cope. I don't feel in control of the situation.*

2 *Marketing director: Listen, I'm having trouble with a major project. I have put together a team of marketing staff from all our different branches, not just here but all over the world, to work together to update our global marketing procedures. The problem is that nobody attends the meetings and progress is slow. Several members have already asked to leave the project.*

Miguel

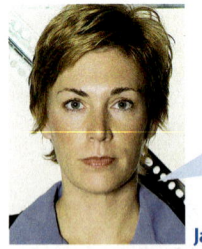

Janet

3 *Departmental manager: I need help with a problem employee. He's making a lot of mistakes and is argumentative with colleagues. What's more, he's taken 20 days' sick leave in the last year and other employees are complaining about it. Several clients have also recently complained about his attitude.*

4 *Project manager: I've been here seven years and I desperately need some training on the latest regulations and accounting procedures in my field. I'm now coordinating an international project and it's embarrassing that I know almost nothing about EU law. My boss tells me we're too busy for training courses, but it's essential that I'm totally up to date. What do you recommend? Can you talk to my boss?*

Holger

Development solutions

a We are so global in our business approaches, I recommend that we introduce team development training for our managers and staff generally. My proposal is to put it on the agenda for the international managers meeting in three weeks' time.

b It's essential that we enable our employees to broaden their professional skills and keep up to date in their field of work. We'll lose staff if we continue to expect them to muddle through without investing in their – and our – future!

c Clearly this should be dealt with by the manager personally! It's high time we introduced a staff appraisal scheme. This is long overdue and will focus managers' minds on the development and evaluation of their employees and hopefully avoid a lot of communication problems like this one.

d In order to avoid problems like this, we need to introduce an induction programme to inform and empower new employees. Maybe we should also look into the benefits of a mentoring scheme too.

VOCABULARY ASSISTANT argumentative *streitsüchtig* to cope *fertigwerden* to empower *ermächtigen* to enable *ermöglichen* field of work *Arbeitsbereich* to muddle through *sich durchwursteln* overdue *überfällig*

Making recommendations

We need to introduce …	It's essential to take up/that we take up
My proposal is to put/is that we put …	references …
Maybe we should also look into …	I (can) recommend talking/that we talk …
I propose introducing/that we introduce …	It's high time (that) we introduced …

3 Study the useful phrases for making recommendations above. Then use the words in the box to complete the sentences below.

> essential • high time • I propose • need to •
> proposal • recommend • we should

1 I _____ hiring this trainer for your appraisal skills training. She's very good.

2 It's _____ we introduced flexible working arrangements for all employees, but it's _____ that client needs are given priority.

3 Obviously we _____ ensure equal opportunities exist throughout the organization first, then maybe _____ also issue a written statement.

4 Having studied the problem and discussed it with my staff, _____ that we postpone the project until next year.

5 My _____ is that we include the information in the next newsletter to all our staff.

4 Now use the language above to make recommendations. Discuss with a partner what HR development you would recommend for these staff problems.

1 A female accountant has complained that her salary is lower than two other male employees who do the same work. She was promoted to the job five years ago, is very well qualified and has been with the company longer than one of the two men.

2 A long-established company has lost some good employees recently because they found it impossible to balance their working lives with the demands of their family life. There is currently no flexitime, very few part-time jobs and only one male employee has taken paternity leave to look after his child due to the negative feeling about such practices.

5 Discuss with a partner.

1 Why do companies introduce appraisal schemes? To improve performance, motivate staff, … ? Brainstorm other reasons. How do you use appraisal in your company?

2 Does your company offer training to managers and team leaders on how to carry out appraisal interviews? If so, what does it involve?

6   **Gaby Meyer, a line manager at Aus-pharma, is carrying out an appraisal interview with Peter Grahame, an employee from the Edinburgh branch who is on secondment in Vienna for two years. Read the dialogue and say what the goal of this appraisal interview is.**

Peter   … Well, my biggest strengths are paying attention to detail and accuracy. Unfortunately, this slows me down and sometimes things get a little behind.

Gaby   How do you see the relationship with your team?

Peter   OK. I don't seem to have any problems there.

Gaby   And the output of your team – tell me about that.

Peter   Well, we were on target for the first three months and then we fell behind because of staff difficulties.

Gaby   To be quite frank, Peter, you were actually 25 per cent down for six months of the year.

Peter   Yes, well, that's because Antonio was on sick leave for so long.

Gaby   I see. When did you realize that his absence would cause problems with meeting targets?

Peter   Well, I knew it would from the beginning.

Gaby   Then could you tell me why you didn't come to see me, Peter?

Peter   You were away on that project in Turkey and I had hoped to solve the problem myself by working overtime. And with the help of Corinna Wielens.

Gaby   So what happened then? Why didn't it work?

Peter   Corinna had problems at home and couldn't put in extra time, and I had too much to do with the day-to-day stuff. No one else was able to do it.

Gaby   With respect, I was only away for a month. Why didn't you raise this issue at the regular team meetings? I'm concerned you didn't feel able to discuss it with me.

Peter   Actually, I prefer to deal with these things myself and you're always busy.

Gaby   But the results are not very impressive, Peter. Your team can't help to resolve the problems if you don't discuss them. You need to think about delegating more to other team members. This will reduce the pressure on yourself. So how do you suggest we go on? How can I help you?

Peter   Well, perhaps we could have another team member until Antonio returns, and maybe I need some training in leadership skills and time management. Actually, there's a bit of a cultural problem with Antonio, too. Before he went sick he was having difficulty dealing with the

Austrian formality and wasn't very happy here. That caused a few problems with other members of the team.

Gaby   OK, well, neither of the first two suggestions should present a problem. I'll talk to our production director this afternoon. And I know about Antonio's problems. He has discussed them with me and we're sending him on some cultural training when he's back. We may do it for all your team as it's such a mixed group. But, I'd like to add one other thing: I think you and I need to improve our communication, Peter, so let's meet weekly for a while and see how we go. OK?

Peter OK. That sounds goods.

Gaby Right. Going back to the question of output, we have to get your team's output up to scratch as soon as possible. I'd like you to arrange a meeting with your team and discuss how you can improve performance in the coming months. OK?

Peter Yes, fine.

Gaby Finally, on a personal note, Peter, how is your wife settling in? I think there were a few problems initially?

Peter Yes, that's right. Actually, she's now found a job in her field – she's a physiotherapist – and she's very happy with it. So that has taken a lot of worry off my shoulders.

7 **Use the words below to complete the appraisal report. Decide on the last two action points yourself.**

communicate • cultural • decrease • delegate • leadership • long-term sickness • production director • overtime • relationships • skills • training manager • to detail

Aus-pharma AG

Appraisal Report

Name: Peter Grahame   **Job title:** Team Leader (bottling)
Appraiser: Gaby Meyer   **Location:** Vienna
Date: 12 December 20..   **Date of last appraisal:** na

Strengths:
Attention _____[1], excellent. Accuracy, good.
Peter feels he doesn't have any problems with staff _____[2].
Wife now in employment of her choice.

Weaknesses:
Peter doesn't always _____[3] to team members and this causes overwork
for himself and thus a _____[4] in output. Communication
_____[5] need attention.

Problems:
Decrease in output caused by Antonio's _____[6], inability of other team
members to work _____[7], shortage of staff in the team. Peter didn't feel
able to _____[8] with me. Antonio needs _____[9] training
(as does all the team!).

Action:
1 Speak to _____[10] about:
   • temporary transfer of member of staff to Peter's team.
   • _____[11] skills and time management training for Peter.
2 Talk to _____[12] about cultural training for all of Peter's team.
3 _____[13].
4 _____[14].

Signed: Appraiser _____   Appraisee _____

8   **Match these expressions from the dialogue with their definitions.**

1   to pay attention to detail
2   to get a little behind
3   to be on target
4   to raise an issue
5   to get sth up to scratch
6   to settle in

a   to make sth as good as it can be
b   to notice and deal with small individual facts
c   to feel happy in a new environment
d   to be at the exact level predicted
e   to mention sth for people to discuss
f   to be slower than expected

BEST PRACTICE

The language of appraisal interviews
The idea of appraisal is to put the wrongs right and then look forward. Questions should always be formulated carefully to avoid upsetting the appraisee during the interview. Being diplomatic and using language to soften disagreement also helps to create a 'positive' environment.

Being diplomatic
- Use 'would', 'could' and 'may' to make statements less direct: *That would/could/may be very difficult.* (Not: *That is very difficult.*)
- Avoid negative words like 'terrible', 'awful', 'very bad'. (Not: *That's a terrible attitude.*) Instead use 'not very' plus a positive word: *That's not a very positive attitude.*

Appraisal questions
Could you tell me (how things are going with ...)?
How do you see (your team developing in ...)?
Would you like to give me more details about ...?

When did you realize that ...?
Would you mind giving me more information on ...?
Is there anything else we should talk about?

Softening disagreement
With respect, I think ...
To be quite frank, Sven, I don't think ...
Frankly, we should deal with that differently ...
I respect your opinion, but ...
I'm afraid we can't / I'm sorry but we can't ...
You have a point there, but ...
To a certain extent I agree, but ...

---

9   **How can you improve these statements and questions from an appraisal interview? Find more diplomatic equivalents in the appraisal dialogue in exercise 6.**

Example: 1   *How do you see the relationship with your team?*

1   *Don't you have a good relationship with your team?*

5   *The results are awful, Peter.*

2   *Your figures were really bad – 25% below target won't do!*

6   *You just have to learn how to delegate more!*

3   *You should have told me.*

7   *Communication with me has to improve immediately, is that clear?*

4   *It's terrible you didn't even tell me about it.*

8   *So Peter – how's the wife – any happier?*

10   Now work with a partner to practise an appraisal interview with a member of staff who is unhappy in his or her job. Either use the profiles in the partner files or think of a situation of your own.

PARTNER FILES   Partner A   File 04, p. 60
Partner B   File 04, p. 62

> **USEFUL PHRASES**
>
> **Asking about the job**
> I'd like you to tell me how you see your progress over the last year.
> Has there been anything you have found difficult to cope with?
> How are things with the rest of the department?
> What do you like most about your work?
>
> **Talking about problems**
> Unfortunately, there have been some problems.
> There seems to be a personality problem between myself and someone in the department.
> Well, actually, someone is making life rather unpleasant for me.
> I didn't feel able to talk to you about it earlier.

11   Match the headings to these short descriptions of four training courses.

Assertive leadership skills

Leadership and team building

Managing your time

Balancing priorities and managing projects

1
Being a competent leader means being able to motivate and get things done. The course includes decision-making, diplomacy and being sensitive to the needs of others.
(8-hour 1-day course)

2
Learn how to set priorities, control your workload and complete tasks on time.
Identify what's important and fulfil targets and objectives more effectively in less time.
(1-day seminar)

3
Successful leaders know how to …
• handle people effectively and get results.
• deal with conflicts and communicate confidently.
• earn the respect of their peer group and their superiors.
(2-day course for managers and supervisors)

4
Prioritize and keep on top of multiple projects, manage conflicting demands and take control over your workload.
Set deadlines and stick to them. Get more done in less time than you thought possible.
(2-day seminar)

Which course would you send Peter Grahame on? Why? Discuss with a partner.

12   Match words from both columns to form word partnerships from the course descriptions above. The first one has been done for you.

1 (competent)   5 to set
2 peer   6 to complete
3 to take   7 to fulfil
4 to get   8 to handle

priorities   control   group
people   results
(leader)   targets   tasks

13 In pairs, design a one-day 'time management' course for a department in your company. Write an introduction as in the examples on page 39 and a short list of the contents. (Try to use a few of the word partnerships in exercise 12.) Present your results and compare with others in the group.

14 Word families: Complete the following sentences with words related to the key words. (You might need to add prefixes or suffixes and change the form.)

equal

1 _____ pay for men and women is still a big issue in some sectors of business.

2 All personnel are subject to the same rules, so everybody is dealt with _____ .

3 The Race Relations Act is about doing away with _____ and discrimination.

appraise

4 If we introduce an _____ scheme, we must offer training on interviewing techniques and managing the scheme.

5 The people doing the interviews are the _____ and the people being assessed are the _____ .

15 Where would you expect to find the following statements written? Do you find similar statements in your company or other companies in your country? What is your reaction to them?

" ... striving to be an equal opportunities employer and service provider. We are working towards a workforce that reflects the wider community and actively encourages job applications from under-represented groups."

"... committed to Equal Opportunities & Investors in People."

" ... offers flexible patterns of work including job-sharing, part-time and short-term contracts and is working towards equality of opportunity for all."

" ... we value having a workforce as diverse as the city we serve. We therefore welcome, develop and promote people from all sections of the community."

" ... our policy is that all people receive equal treatment regardless of their sex, marital status, sexuality, race, creed, colour, ethnic or national origin, or disability."

VOCABULARY ASSISTANT

committed *engagiert*
creed *Glaube*
ethnic origin *Herkunft*

CLOCK-OUT

Read the following article from an equal opportunities website.

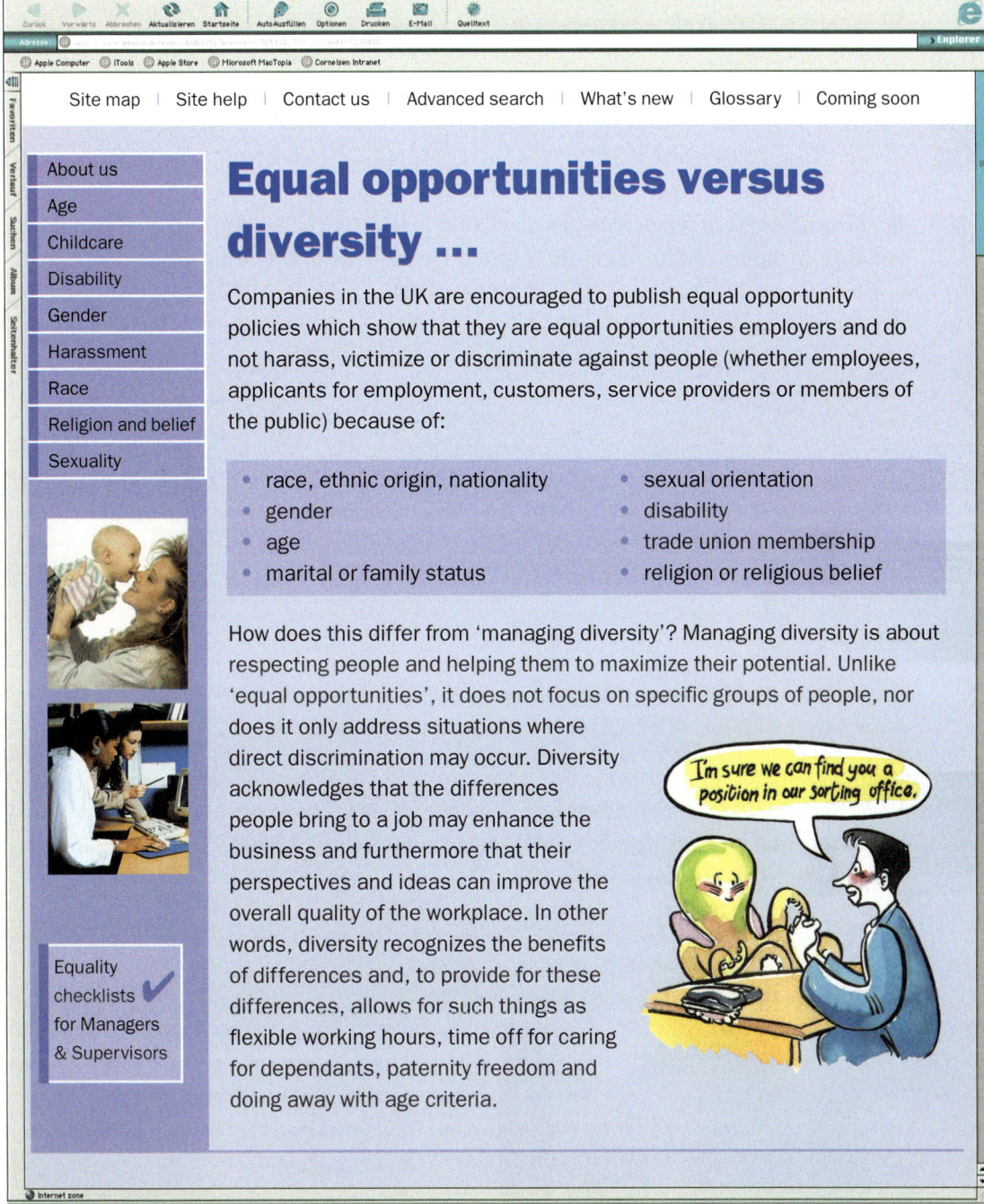

Site map | Site help | Contact us | Advanced search | What's new | Glossary | Coming soon

About us
Age
Childcare
Disability
Gender
Harassment
Race
Religion and belief
Sexuality

Equal opportunities versus diversity …

Companies in the UK are encouraged to publish equal opportunity policies which show that they are equal opportunities employers and do not harass, victimize or discriminate against people (whether employees, applicants for employment, customers, service providers or members of the public) because of:

- race, ethnic origin, nationality
- gender
- age
- marital or family status
- sexual orientation
- disability
- trade union membership
- religion or religious belief

How does this differ from 'managing diversity'? Managing diversity is about respecting people and helping them to maximize their potential. Unlike 'equal opportunities', it does not focus on specific groups of people, nor does it only address situations where direct discrimination may occur. Diversity acknowledges that the differences people bring to a job may enhance the business and furthermore that their perspectives and ideas can improve the overall quality of the workplace. In other words, diversity recognizes the benefits of differences and, to provide for these differences, allows for such things as flexible working hours, time off for caring for dependants, paternity freedom and doing away with age criteria.

I'm sure we can find you a position in our sorting office.

Equality checklists ✔ for Managers & Supervisors

OVER TO YOU

According to the article, what is the reason for publishing equal opportunity statements?
Do you think such statements add value to the reputation of a company?
How many companies that you know of are actively involved in diversity? How is it dealt with in your organization?

5 Reward and remuneration

Benefits (ie rewards companies give their staff in addition to money) are often called 'fringe benefits' or 'perks'. Add as many different fringe benefits to this mind map as you can.

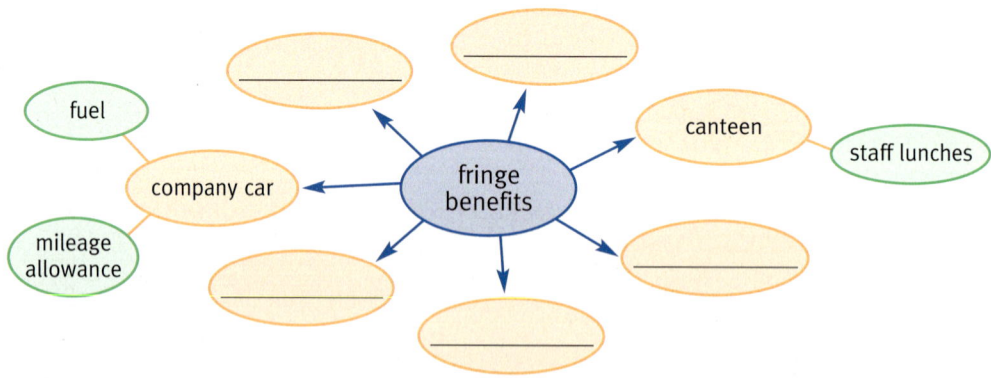

Do you think staff are more motivated by receiving a higher salary with fewer benefits or a lower basic salary with lots of benefits? Discuss with your colleagues.

1 **Heike Schuett, the personnel manager of an international company in Frankfurt, is having a departmental meeting with her staff, Paola Canarutto and Sven Moritz, about benefits. Which benefits do they mention?**

Heike As you know, we need to review our benefits package to bring it in line with our offices in Denmark and the Netherlands. What is your view on this? Paola?

Paola Yes, I think we need to introduce more family-friendly benefits and also flexible working

hours. Too many staff are working overtime and having problems with their work / life balance.

Heike Could I have your input, Sven?

Sven Uh, yes. What exactly do you mean by work/life balance, Paola?

Paola It means trying to achieve a better balance between work and home life.

Sven I see. Well, I'm definitely in favour of flexible working hours. However, I think we should also look closely at childcare – and even eldercare – provisions to encourage some of our female staff back to work. In fact I'd like to submit a proposal on this at a future meeting.

Heike   Good idea. How much time do you need? Could you submit something at our regular meeting in a fortnight?

Sven   That's fine.

Heike   Paola, could you please prepare a summary of all our current benefits and ask accounts to print off a list of the annual costs? These subjects are high on the agenda at the next international meeting in Zurich and I'd like us to have some good input for the meeting.

Paola   Yes, OK. By the way, I've had several discussions with our colleagues in Amsterdam and Copenhagen on their ideas for new initiatives on flexible working, so I'll fill you in on that, too.

Heike   Good. And I'll give you the details of the new profit-sharing bonus the directors have been discussing …

> **DID YOU KNOW?**
>
> Another term for 'pay' or 'salary' is 'remuneration' or 'compensation'.
> A 'remuneration package' is the total of all financial and non-financial benefits an employee receives (ie the salary plus a car, a pension scheme and life assurance).

2   **Use the switchboard to make true statements about the dialogue.**

1   Heike called the meeting   talked to   the new profit-sharing bonus at their next meeting.
2   Paola felt they needed   to discuss   colleagues in other offices about flexitime initiatives.

3   Sven was in favour of   to prepare   more flexibility for staff.
4   He was keen to   giving   a summary of benefits and costs.
5   Sven will prepare a proposal   to inform Paola and Sven about   employees greater freedom to have a good work/life balance.
6   Heike asked Paola   to submit   their benefits package.
7   Paola has already   encourage   female staff back to work.
8   Heike is going   to introduce   at the next regular meeting.

3   **Complete these phrases from the dialogue.**

> **USEFUL PHRASES**
>
> **Asking for somebody's opinion or ideas**
> What is your view on this?
> Could I have some feedback?
> Could _____ [1], Sven?
> _____ [2] prepare a summary …?
>
> **Clarifying**
> What exactly _____ [3] by …?
> As _____ [4], we need …
> I'll fill you in on …
>
> **Giving an opinion or feedback**
> Yes, I think we need …
> Well, I'm _____ [5] of …
> Good idea.
> However, _____ [6] look …
> That's _____ [7].
> By the way, …

4 Two companies have posted their remuneration packages on the job page of their company websites. Label the descriptions of benefits (1–12) with items a–l.

a performance-related pay
b sports club membership
c employee assistance programme
d flexible working hours
e relocation expenses
f pension scheme

g profit-sharing bonus scheme
h life insurance
i cafeteria
j creche / childcare facilities
k shares in success
l salaries

Benefits & rewards

We want to attract, motivate and hold on to our best personnel by rewarding you fairly with the following benefits:

☐ 1 A first-class non-contributory retirement scheme (ie fully paid by the employer).

☐ 2 Coverage for your loved ones of four times your annual salary.

☐ 3 Free shares after one year's service, dependent on company profits.

☐ 4 Fitness, sports facilities, massage and yoga classes plus 20% off membership of a wide selection of fitness clubs.

☐ 5 Daily nursery / kindergarten provision.

☐ 6 Counselling and advice on personal and domestic issues.

Remuneration package

In return for your contribution to our organization, you can expect a role that offers considerable variety and a chance to pursue your ambitions with the company both nationwide and internationally.

○ 7 Depending on level, role and experience, we offer attractive salary packages to recruit and retain the best personnel.

○ 8 Payment is reviewed on a merit basis, based on how well you carry out your job.

○ 9 You can adjust working hours to suit personal and family commitments.

○ 10 Paid out twice a year dependent upon business results.

○ 11 Hot meals, salads and snacks at heavily subsidized prices.

○ 12 Comprehensive moving expenses if you take up a new position or are transferred.

Which package do you find more attractive? Why?

5 Use the clues to complete the puzzle and find the hidden word.

1 you don't have to pay anything: non-...
2 a place where children are looked after
3 money received regularly after retirement
4 a small part of a company which is bought or given as an investment
5 an informal restaurant where you take the food to the table yourself
6 according to how good you are: on a ... basis
7 moving an employee to a new worksite
8 giving professional advice

6 Word families: Complete the following sentences with words related to the key words. (You might need to add prefixes or suffixes and change the form.)

benefit

1 We all _____ greatly from job satisfaction.

2 People receive sickness and unemployment _____ from the State.

3 Your husband is the _____ of your life assurance policy in the event of your death.

review

4 Salaries are normally _____ annually.

5 We carry out appraisal or performance _____ in September/October each year.

7 Now use phrases from page 43 and below to role-play a meeting with your colleague(s) about benefit packages. Either refer to the role cards in the partner files or think of your own situation.

PARTNER FILES Partner A   File 05, p. 61
Partner B   File 05, p. 63
Partner B1 File 07, p. 63

USEFUL PHRASES

Agreeing and disagreeing
I entirely agree.
I'm inclined to agree with you on that.
Yes, but have you considered ...?
I'm afraid I can't go along with that.
Sorry, but I really can't agree.

Interrupting
Could I just say that ...?
I'd like to add a point here.
Excuse me, can I just come in here?
Sorry, but may I just clarify a point before we go on?

8   **You are writing a short follow-up email to the Board about your recommendations. Choose the correct words in each sentence, then put the sentences in the right order.**

Dear Board Members

a   Best wishes/Yours faithfully [1]
Remuneration Committee

b   We appreciate that it will be necessary to hold a detailed meeting about this, but we look forward to hearing your initial/prompt [2] comments.

c   We would like to recommend/recommending [3] that the attached proposals be introduced over the next two years.

d   If you require any further information/informations [4], please let us know.

e   At a meeting of/from [5] the Remuneration Committee last week, the question of a new benefits package has been/was [6] raised.

f   We feel this would offer/involve [7] the staff more flexible working arrangements, while benefiting the company in terms of a happy and contented workforce/workers [8].

9   **Heike is now talking to the marketing manager, Tim Brown, about salary increases for his staff. As you read, find words you can use to talk about trends and put them in the table.**

upward movement	downward movement
an increase	

Heike   As you know, we haven't reviewed salaries for over a year. The Board has agreed a maximum 5% increase from 1 October and I'd like you to come back to me with recommendations for all your staff. I've produced a list here with the relevant data about each employee in Marketing.

Tim   That's fine. I've got one or two people who deserve more than 5%, particularly those who came from London and New York last year. They actually took a drop in salary and they've reminded me about this several times. It's eighteen months since we had our last raise, too.

Heike   Well, we might be able to give more in one or two cases if you reward less in others. Don't forget the rate of inflation is not expected to rise much in Germany this year and so far, touch wood, we haven't had to make any staff redundant.

Tim   What's the position likely to be on the bonuses at the end of the year? Will they be slashed? And are there any other staff developments on the horizon?

Heike   Well, we are proposing to carry out the performance reviews in November and early December and that will determine the final bonus amounts. We're trying to separate the salary review from the performance review in future. We're also looking at flexible working and maternity and childcare issues. Your department is particularly vulnerable here as you have less staff and therefore a number of people who work too many hours. Also, there are several women on maternity leave at present who I believe you would like back. Frankly, Tim, I'm worried about the number of hours some of your staff are working. It has to be contained.

Tim   OK, I hope we'll have the opportunity to discuss some of these issues at the management meeting. Thanks, Heike. I'll get back to you within a week.

DID YOU KNOW?

In the UK a salary increase is also called 'a rise'. It is called 'a raise' in the USA.

VOCABULARY ASSISTANT

to contain   *unter Kontrolle bringen*
on the horizon   *in Sicht*   to slash   *(drastisch) reduzieren*   to be vulnerable   *in einer prekären Lage sein*

10   **Look at Tim's notes from the meeting and correct them where necessary.**

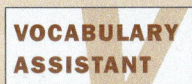

   1 The Board ~~needs to agree~~ *has agreed* the ~~5.5%~~ *5%* review, effective from 1 October.

   2 I told Heike that there are at least six staff who should get more than 5% (those who relocated from Canada last year).

   3 Performance review and salary review will be separated in future.

   Tell staff

   4 There won't be any redundancies this year.

   5 Performance reviews will take place in the new year.

   6 Flexitime will be introduced next year.

   7 No figure for next year's bonuses yet.

   Action

   8 Give Heike my recommendations asap.

   9 Keep reviews to the agreed level if possible.

Talking about figures and numbers

Figures and numbers are used extensively in human resources to talk about salaries, bonuses and budgets. The following abbreviations are commonly used in writing:

k	thousand	€50 k *(fifty thousand euros)*
m	million	$10 m *(ten million dollars)*
bn	billion	£5.75 bn *(five point seven five billion pounds)*
inc	including	€25,000 (inc benefits) *(twenty-five thousand euros, including benefits)*.
ph	per hour	$10.00 ph *(ten dollars per hour)*
pa	per annum	€20,000 pa *(twenty thousand euros per annum)*

Note the differences:

459	four hundred *and* fifty-nine (UK)		45,000	(Not: ~~45.000~~)
	four hundred fifty-nine (US)		$8.75	(Not: ~~$8,75~~)

11 **How do you say these figures? Say them or write them out in full.**

1 €5000 3 $50,239,150 5 $110,000,000

2 £60,000 pa 4 €70 bn 6 £150 ph

12 **In the UK it is usual to quote salaries when advertising jobs. Match the salaries or wages below (1–6) with the extracts from job adverts (a–f). How do these salaries and hourly rates compare to those in your country?**

1 Salary approx. £18,000 pa

2 £45,724 – £48,750 pa – a relocation package is available

3 £8.00 per inspection

4 £4 per hour (rising to £4.40 per hour after 12 weeks)

5 £8.00 ph Monday to Saturday / £10.00 ph Sunday and bank holidays

6 Salary £50,000 + car + extensive benefits

a
Vehicle Inspectors
Use your own car to look at the vehicles of prospective insurance customers and complete a simple checklist. Pay according to how many inspections you carry out. Ideal candidate must have own car, hold a full driving licence …

b
Customer Service Assistants
We are currently seeking people with previous customer service experience, who can work flexible shifts. The job involves dealing with our customers at the airport, giving advice, recommending products and offering travel tips …

c
Now recruiting bus drivers …
Full-time vacancies available for PCV licence holders. You will benefit from 4 weeks' paid holiday, pension scheme and free travel on bus and underground services …

d
Head of Personnel Services
One of the oldest police forces in the country with ca. 2300 staff, with an excellent reputation for performance, seeks an experienced HR professional to lead an HR team across the county …

e

Electricians

Productivity bonus, 40 hours per week, vehicle supplied. Applications are invited from experienced and qualified electricians to join our busy team. Please apply for a recruitment pack by phoning …

f

UK Sales Manager, Essex

required to lead the UK sales force. At least five years' successful experience in a similar post in the food and beverage sector is a must. Excellent communication skills, a flair for business and a competitive spirit are essential …

DID YOU KNOW?

'Wage' was traditionally used for the money paid regularly to a worker (usually in cash on a weekly basis) and 'salary' for monthly pay. However 'wage' is still used as an alternative to 'salary' when talking about 'pay' in general, eg 'wage differentials', 'wage freeze', 'minimum wage'.

CLOCK-OUT

Read this article from an HR trade magazine and discuss the questions which follow.

Dissatisfaction over benefits packages

 Companies are wasting billions providing non-salary benefits, the value of which is not understood by employees

New research has revealed that many employees don't appreciate their benefits or know their value in monetary terms, despite the fact that 90% of employers believe such benefits are essential to both attract and keep staff.

At a time of strong competition in the recruitment market, it's essential that money is spent on relevant benefits and that they are appreciated by the staff. There is a move towards more flexible benefits where employees can choose their package, the report stated. A number of initiatives are currently being piloted by companies.

One such company recently decided to introduce a new benefits package in stages and then issued all staff with an employee benefits statement, so they could see exactly what they were getting. Now they are running focus groups on the scheme, before introducing fully flexible benefits. These focus groups allow staff and employers to examine the full extent of the benefits being offered, and to find out which benefits have the most value to each individual and how they can best help the work/life balance of today's employees.

Is this being too democratic? As long as budgets are not exceeded, what could be better than to consult with employees on what benefits they prefer? You could have a more contented and motivated workforce at the end of the day.

OVER TO YOU

What fringe benefits, if any, are negotiable in your company? Are new employees ever asked what benefits they would prefer to have?

6 Industrial relations

CLOCK-IN

How much do you know about trade unions? Discuss the following statements with a partner and correct any that you think are false. Do others in the group agree with you?

1 European countries with the highest strike rates are Spain, Greece and Finland.
2 Trade unions are called 'labor unions' in the US.
3 The largest union in Germany is IG Metall.
4 A 'closed shop' is common in some large industrial sectors in the UK. It's illegal in Germany.
5 Sweden's largest union represents more than 1/5 of the country's population – 2.1 m members.
6 The main purpose of a trade union is to look after the interests of employers.
7 The umbrella organization for all German unions is the DGB, Deutscher Gewerkschaftsbund.
8 Austria's biggest industrial action for nearly 60 years took place in 2003 when more than 1 m workers went on strike over a reduction in unemployment benefits.

> **DID YOU KNOW?**
>
> 'Closed shop' (*gewerkschaftspflichtiger Betrieb*) means a company can engage only employees who belong to the union.

1 **Work with a partner. What do you think the following headlines are about?**

> **German court supports Sunday closing law**

> **Finance workers in Denmark anxious over bank security**

> **Ver.di turns up the heat in wage negotiations with Deutsche Post**

Now read the summaries of the three stories behind the headlines to see if you were right. Find words or phrases which mean the following:

1 fighting for something
2 a worldwide plan
3 an arrangement made between management and union representatives
4 an offer made by somebody who has rejected a previous offer

A Germany's Federal Constitutional Court has refused to allow shops to open on Sundays. Rest on Sundays and national holidays is considered more important than the economic interests of businesses, says the court. Ver.di had supported this decision and, together with church groups, had been campaigning to keep Sunday a day of rest.

B The leader of the finance workers' union has called for national and European action to make workplaces more secure. Thousands of bank staff have been victims of bank robberies (an average of one a day in Denmark), with many requiring post traumatic stress treatment. He encouraged unions and employers to work together in a global initiative for safer workplaces.

C In ongoing negotiations to renew the collective agreement for German postal workers, Deutsche Post AG has not yet put forward a counter-offer to ver.di for better income conditions. Ver.di is seeking a 4% increase in wages and has called for local strikes to put pressure on the company.

2 **Put the phrases below into the right word order. Then use them to complete the sentences.**

a a shop closed enforce _enforce a closed shop_ _____

b conditions pay and negotiate _____

c take action industrial _____

d interests after look employees' _____

e wage involved be in negotiations _____

f agreement collective discuss a _____

g offer put a counter- forward _____

1 The Personnel Manager is going to _____ to the union of a 5% pay rise.

2 Each year we have to _____ with the union representatives.

3 The major publishing company had no choice but to _enforce a closed shop_____ .

4 The workers threatened to _____ if the redundancies went ahead.

5 In the UK, shop stewards are elected by union members to _____ _____ and represent them to management.

6 Legislation lays down minimum time periods for consultation to _____ _____ when more than 20 redundancies are proposed.

7 The company will soon _____ with the union.

DID YOU KNOW?

Non-union companies in the UK do not have an official or a recognized joint employee consultation system like the German *Betriebsrat* (works council). Unionized companies have 'shop stewards' (or 'union representatives') who have been elected by union members to represent them to management. Thus they are a sort of combination of German works council members and trade union negotiators.

3 Klaus Bohn, the personnel manager of an international company in Cologne, is meeting with Jason Hughes, the industrial relations manager of their plant in the UK. Which statement best describes the situation they are discussing?

a Workers at the plant are on strike.

b Workers at the plant are dissatisfied with the proposed wage increase.

c Workers at the plant are concerned about safety issues.

Jason I'm afraid we've got a problem, Klaus. The 3% increase Management agreed for the plant has been rejected by the Union.

Klaus Oh! What's behind it?

Jason They want the same increase as the white-collar staff – at least 5%. The union representatives held a meeting with their members last night and failed to reach agreement.

Klaus What was your counter-argument?

Jason We haven't had an official meeting yet – that will be next week. But I told them that sales were down and that if things got worse, we might have to think about some redundancies in Amsterdam. I also reminded them that they had a 3% review a year ago.

Klaus Did you know that the white-collar staff haven't had a review in salary for two years now? We froze their salaries because we had lost a huge contract and then there was the recession, but we decided to review the shop-floor workers to avoid industrial action. All this happened just before you joined.

Jason I see. Well, I know they want at least 5%. It appears there have been rumours of an economic downturn in the industry and the transfer of work to the Polish subsidiary. So of course the staff are nervous about the future of the plant. Despite this, they still feel 3% is too low and doesn't compensate them for loss of overtime over the last six months.

Klaus It doesn't make any sense. But I must say I thought it might happen.

Jason We've got to plan our tactics. We can't offer 5%, that's for sure, but we don't want any strikes at present. Let's talk to the management committee again before the meeting.

4 Fill in the missing words in each of the questions below. Then use information from the dialogue to answer the questions.

1 What's *b*_____ the union's rejection of the pay deal?

2 What exactly was Jason's *c*_____-argument?

3 Why did the union representatives and their members *f*_____ to reach *a*_____?

4   Why did they _f_____ the salaries of white-collar staff two years ago?

5   What are the _r_____ going around the plant?

6   Why have Klaus and Jason got to plan their _t_____?

It looks as if there could be a long and difficult negotiation with the union representing the workers at the British plant. How can companies avoid situations like this?

5   **Which phrase in each pair matches the definition (1–6)?**

1   to reject a proposal or suggestion
  a   to make a counter-offer
  b   to fail to reach agreement

2   workers on the production line
  a   blue-collar workers
  b   white-collar workers

3   a general fall in orders across many business sectors
  a   when productivity is down
  b   an economic downturn

4   a response to another suggestion
  a   a counter-argument
  b   a negotiation

5   the place where the goods are produced
  a   the plant
  b   the shop floor

6   to stop pay for a certain period
  a   to freeze salaries
  b   to negotiate a new pay deal

6   **What makes a successful negotiation? Work with a partner to rank the tips below from 1–10 (1 being the most important). Can you add any more tips to the list?**

☐ Always listen carefully to the other person.

☐ Be flexible and prepared to compromise.

☐ Be positive – highlight the 'common ground'.

☐ Build rapport and be courteous.

☐ Use simple and clear language.

☐ Use persuasion, not threats.

☐ Prepare your arguments.

☐ Be constructive and avoid open conflict.

☐ Always remember your aims.

☐ When agreement is reached, summarize clearly and close the deal.

7 **Match the following sentences to the five parts of a negotiation. Check your answers with a partner.**

building rapport ☐ ☐   addressing conflict ☐ ☐

establishing objectives and aims ☐ ☐   concluding ☐1☐ ☐

bargaining ☐ ☐

1 Excellent, then let me conclude by summing up the meeting.
2 If the white-collar workers accepted a pay freeze last year, it's not unreasonable to give them a higher increase now.
3 Let's not get too hot under the collar.
4 We'd like to start by welcoming everyone and restating our proposals.
5 Believe me, we'd really like to shake hands and walk out of here today with a positive result.
6 But we want your assurances that there will be no industrial action.
7 We are happy to meet you today to work out a solution.
8 That's it, then. A successful conclusion for everybody.
9 We've studied the figures and the bottom line is that there's not much money in the pot, so we have to reach a compromise!
10 Management has asked us to give you their assurances on this point.

8 **Jason Hughes and Klaus Bohn are now meeting the union representatives, among them Helen Barker and Bob Cage, to try to reach agreement on the pay deal. Which sentences from exercise 7 do they say?**

Jason Thank you for calling the meeting. We are happy to meet you today to work out a solution. We'd like to start by welcoming everyone and restating our proposals. Then perhaps you could outline why the offer was rejected by your members. Klaus?

Klaus Yes. A 3% increase has been agreed, which we consider is a reasonable and fair offer given the current economic situation and the fact that our sales are down. The outlook isn't a very bright one at present, but we think things will improve in the next six to nine months provided we can contain costs. I'd also like to remind you that you had a 3% review a year ago while the salaries of the white-collar workers were frozen.

Helen But our members aren't happy with 3% and, since overtime was stopped six months ago, they feel they have suffered enough. It's a difficult situation, that's true, but they want a minimum of 5%. What's more, they are threatening industrial action if they don't get it.

Jason That's a bit unfair, isn't it? I heard there are some rumours going around about transferring work to a Polish subsidiary. Has this got anything to do with it?

Bob Yes, that's right. They are worried that the plant is facing closure. That would be a disaster for an area like this which is already facing high unemployment. You know what rumours are like.

Klaus We'd like to reassure you that, as far as we are aware, there is no plan to close the plant or transfer business to Poland. Management has asked us to give you their assurances on this point. We've studied the figures and the bottom line is that there's not much money in the pot, so we have to reach a compromise!

Bob   I'm sorry, but why should we believe this? Outsourcing is happening everywhere at present – cheaper labour, cheaper factories …

Jason   Let's not get too hot under the collar, Bob. We consider ourselves to be a fair and reasonable employer with a consistent record of commitment and honesty with our employees. There's also the Dutch plant to consider. As I mentioned when we met before, if sales continue to fall in Amsterdam, we'll have a big problem there. We think we can deal with it, but if we have to pay out more money here, then it's unlikely we can. Listen, we'd like to put our cards on the table. If your members accept 3% now, we will give a further $1\frac{1}{2}$% in nine months, as long as there isn't a substantial drop in sales. But we want your assurances that there will be no industrial action.

Helen   Could we have ten minutes to talk about it outside?

Jason   Certainly. Let's break for coffee and meet back in 20 minutes …

* * *

Helen   OK. We think this is a reasonable compromise. Our members will agree 3% now and $1\frac{1}{2}$% in nine months. And you have our assurances there will be no industrial action.

Klaus   That's it then. A successful conclusion for everybody. Thank you.

Jason   Good, I'll send you written confirmation tomorrow, which you can post on the notice boards around the shop floor if you like. The 3% review will take effect from 1 March.

> **VOCABULARY ASSISTANT**
>
> closure *Schließung*   hot under the collar *wütend*   to take effect *in Kraft treten*   threat/to threaten *Drohung/drohen*

9 After the meeting, Jason writes the following email to the management committee. Complete the gaps with the correct form of the verbs below.

> accept • be • give • meet • not be (2x) • receive • transfer

Dear Management Committee

As you know, Klaus Bohn and I _____ ¹ with the union representatives last night to discuss their rejection of the pay offer of 3%, effective 1 March and the threat of industrial action. Apart from the fact that white-collar workers _____ ² 5%, there _____ ³, as I suspected, strong rumours going round that we're closing the plant and _____ ⁴ work to Poland.

We _____ ⁵ the union representatives our assurances that this _____ ⁶ the case and agreed the 3% increase from 1 March, followed by a further $1\frac{1}{2}$% in nine months, as long as there _____ ⁷ a substantial fall in sales and provided that there is no industrial action. They _____ ⁸ the offer on behalf of their members.

We feel this is a successful conclusion to the negotiations.

Best wishes
Jason Hughes

What types of negotiations have you been involved in? Describe your experiences to your colleagues.

BEST PRACTICE

The language of negotiating

A negotiation is often a very delicate procedure where even the language you use can influence the outcome. While diplomatic language (see page 38) and building rapport are both essential for keeping the negotiation polite and friendly, there are also many fixed phrases which can help make finding the right words easier. Below are some typical phrases for persuading and bargaining.

Persuading

It would be to your advantage to …
If might be in your interest to …
We can reassure you on that point totally.
It's the best offer around. You won't find a better one.

If you stopped picketing, then I think we could make a counter-offer.
We might put a better offer on the table, **provided (that)** you stop the strike.
I'd go along with that **on condition that** you returned to work.
That seems a good compromise, **as long as** as there is no industrial action of any kind.
Unless your members return to normal working tomorrow, we'll withdraw our offer.

Bargaining

We would agree on one condition.
If you agree to …, we can …
If you threathen us, we'll withdraw the offer.

10 **Use the key words in brackets to make complete sentences about the conditions and offers below. The first sentence has been done for you.**

1 our members get 5% increase in pay/take industrial action *(unless)*
   Unless our members get a 5% increase in pay they will take industrial action.

2 be an increase in sales/can offer further 2% pay rise *(provided that)*
   _____

3 no further increases in pay/be no job losses Amsterdam *(if/will)*
   _____

4 another review in nine months/no industrial action *(on condition that)*
   _____

5 productivity increased/pay a bonus end of the year *(if/could)*
   _____

6 open on Sundays from 10–4 pm/lose business to competitors *(unless)*
   _____

7 customer service not suffer/introduce flexible working hours *(provided)*
   _____

11 **Work with a partner. Choose a few situations below – or think of your own – and try to persuade your partner to accept your position. Be prepared to bargain.**

1 You've referred several people for a secretarial position. You feel that one candidate is clearly the best but the manager prefers another person.
2 You need two staff to work at the weekend.
3 You'd like to take four of your six weeks' holiday together this year. (The rule is a maximum of two weeks at a time.)
4 Your post room now needs to work a two-shift day: 5 am–1 pm and 1 pm–9 pm. The staff are not happy about this.
5 An employee has decided to leave the company. You need to convince him/her to stay.

12   **Word families: Complete the following sentences with words related to the key words.**
(You might need to add prefixes or suffixes and change the form.)

negotiate

1   Jason Hughes has an excellent record as a first-class _____ .

2   The offer we made to the union was not _____ .

3   The next _____ on pay and conditions takes place on 1 September.

consult

4   We use a very experienced _____ from a firm of industrial mediators when we have a tough problem with the union.

5   Our joint _____ committee meets twice a year.

6   _____ with the union can be difficult at the best of times!

13   **Work with a partner to do a role-play. First look at the tips and the phrases in this unit.**
Then use the role cards in the partner files or think up your own situation to negotiate with
your partner.

PARTNER FILES   Partner A   File 06, p. 61
Partner B   File 06, p. 63

CLOCK-OUT

Has your company ever outsourced any jobs? What was the reaction of your staff?
Read the following extracts and discuss with the rest of the group.

A major German supermarket chain plans to outsource 350 jobs for software professionals to India. The plan is to have approximately 650 staff in its Indian subsidiary by the end of 2005. Originally the chain gave assurances that the move would not lead to widespread job losses.

1500 steel workers in Sweden were informed their jobs were safe after a major deal with a Finnish-led metal consortium was finalized. Workers welcomed the news as there had been widespread rumours that the plant would be closed.

Two unions have voted against strike action over the closure of a Coventry car plant in the UK. This will lead to a loss of 900 jobs. Despite a protest march in September, workers were urged by their employers not to take strike action as it would not be 'in the interests of the employees, customers and the company'.

Experts at the National Outsourcing Association state that companies will be more open with staff and unions in the future about outsourcing plans, following strike action at various organizations last year. Union consultation should be introduced as early as possible in an effort to avert industrial disputes, it stated ...

OVER TO YOU

What action would you take in such cases, whether unionized or not, to prevent rumours and possible industrial action? Exactly how much of a commitment should an employer have to its staff?

Test yourself!

Across

1 what you write to an unsuccessful candidate: ... letter
5 to move to a new area with your job
9 a programme for new staff to help them settle into a company
11 when you don't have a job, you're ...
15 a shorter word for 'fringe benefits'
19 a way of asking applicants for information at an interview so that they can't just give 'yes/no' answers: ... questions
20 the regular evaluation of an employee's performance and potential
22 written or verbal comments on an employee's character and job performance (in a previous job)
23 in American English it is called a 'raise'
25 being able to maintain a reasonable level of commitment between work and private life: work/life ...
27 same salary or wage for men and women in the same job (two words)
28 valuing the differences between people to maximize potential
29 the time a woman is away from the office to have a baby: ... leave
30 initial period of employment during which an employee is not yet considered permanent: ... period

Down

1 total financial and non-financial benefits an employee gets: ... package
2 the English word for *Betriebsrat*: works ...
3 unpleasant or offensive behaviour towards someone
4 the opposite of 'specialist'
6 disagreement between people
7 being able to choose a starting and finishing time each day as long as total hours are worked
8 a specified period of time in a contract for telling a company an employee is leaving: ... period
10 details of the content of a job and the skills needed for it: job ...
12 working longer hours than your normal contract
13 ways of warning staff that they are breaking rules: ... procedures
14 extra money for working shifts: shift ...
16 goods are produced here (two words)
17 treating people differently because of race, age, sex, colour, etc
18 another word for 'applicant'
21 a complaint about being treated unfairly
24 if you can only hire employees who are union members: ... shop
26 written details of terms and conditions of work: ... contract

Unit 1, Exercise 14   File 01

You are a personnel officer in the head office of an international company. You are visiting one of your European branches and are meeting with Partner B, who is a manager there, to discuss recruiting a new marketing manager. Note the following arguments:
- You want to use a specialist recruitment agency because they can search for the right candidates in various countries and cover a much wider area than an advert in the paper. Also, they can conduct initial interviews and thus save you time.
- Advertising in the national press is expensive and there is more of a risk that you won't find the right candidate.
- As far as you know, there are no existing staff with the right level of experience for this position.

Ask for Partner B's suggestions and give feedback. Try to agree on how you should recruit for this job.

Unit 2, Exercise 8   File 02

You are Melanie Smith. You have applied for a job as Team Leader at the London call centre for Mobile plus GmbH and have just received the letter on page 17. Today is Monday, 28 August. Call Jenny Mills, Personnel Assistant, in London to arrange a convenient date and time for an interview this week or next. Look at your diary and your notes before making the phone call.

AUGUST / SEPTEMBER						
Monday	Tuesday	Wednesday	Thursday	Friday	Saturday	Sunday
28 Meeting 2–6 pm	29	30	31 Night shift 10 pm–6 am	1	2	3
4 Dentist appt 4 pm	5	6 Training course, Reading	7	8	9	10 To South Africa

Notes for telephone call to Jenny Mills
- can't make next week – running training course
- holiday 10–24 Sept (taking children to visit parents) – conflict with assessment centre?!
- directions to office?
- parking?

Unit 3, Exercise 9   File 03

You are Stefan/Stefanie Brinkmann, a personnel officer at the German subsidiary of Greenman International Books, which is located in Stuttgart. You are currently looking for somebody for the position of bookkeeper and are meeting with Frank/Francis Murphy – your best candidate so far – to discuss the terms and conditions of employment. Note that the job requires someone with fluent German (spoken and written) but you are prepared to pay for German lessons. The applicant lives in Stuttgart so there is no relocation involved. Use the notes below to conduct the interview:

hours (no flexitime)
holidays
sickness
benefits
German language training twice a week

Unit 4, Exercise 10   File 04

You are a recruitment officer in a large HR department and are getting ready for your first appraisal interview with your boss – the personnel officer in charge of recruitment.

You've been with the company for one year now (including the six-month probationary period). You started off well in the job and were very happy – it's a challenging post with lots of contact with other branches. In preparation for the appraisal interview, make notes of some of the things you feel you do well and which make you suitable for the position.

Strengths
1 six years' recruiting experience in previous company
2 attention to detail
3
4

Although you like your job, lately you have been thinking about looking for a new position. The reason is that one of your colleagues (Becker) has been making things unpleasant for you for the last 4–5 months. (She/He comments on your work, removes paperwork from your desk, talks about you behind your back, etc.) You feel in a difficult position and have even been to a doctor for stress-related problems.

Prepare what you want to say, then take part in the appraisal interview with your superior. (He/She talked to you briefly some months ago about your performance, but you decided not to go into details at that time.) Then swap roles and do the interview again.

Unit 5, Exercise 7   File 05

As members of the remuneration committee, you and two colleagues are meeting to discuss a new benefits package for your company. You have agreed to chair (leiten) the meeting, so first you need to use these notes from the last meeting to prepare the agenda.

Draft agenda
- *Most important benefits?*
  a *flexible working hours essential*
  b *childcare facilities needed to encourage female employees back to work*
  c *some sort of profit-sharing bonus??*

- *Conclusions and recommendations (should we look at health and sports club issues?)*

You think flexible working hours are essential so prepare a list of what you propose exactly (flexitime /create part-time jobs/job-sharing in some areas?). You would also like to recommend some sports/health-related benefits; decide what this could be (club memberships, massage, sauna?).
Start the meeting by introducing the agenda and then discuss with your colleagues the various benefits that have been recommended. Try to agree on the next steps. (You think you need to go slowly on this – you won't be able to make a decision today. Perhaps you need to first ask the staff what benefits packages *they* would like to have, meet again, then make a proposal to the Board.)

Unit 6, Exercise 13   File 06

Your company has decided to make five IT staff redundant, as the whole IT department is being outsourced to an IT consulting company.
You are a senior member of the HR department and are meeting with a member of the works council to get their agreement, which you need in order to go ahead with the plan. Prepare for the meeting by completing the notes below. You might also want to think of some other arguments. (You expect this to be a difficult meeting as you know there have been some bad rumours going around.)

Meeting – IT redundancies
- cost saving €_____ pa to outsource IT
- four of the five employees will be offered contracts with the IT consulting company
- the new consulting company offers 24-hour per day in-house IT cover (not 15 hrs as at present)
- three of the redundant staff have 10–12 years' service and two joined in the last five months. (still completing their probationary period – not normally subject to redundancy laws so company is being generous).
- you will offer the employees the following leaving package (compensation):
  –
  –
  –

Partner files

Unit 1, Exercise 14   File 01

You are the manager of a European branch of an international company. A personnel officer from your head office (Partner A) is visiting you to discuss recruitment for the job of marketing manager at your branch office. This is what you think:

• You would like to advertise in the national press and deal with the applications yourself, as this is the usual procedure in your country. (Recruitment agencies don't have a very high profile here and don't know your company like you do.)
• There is somebody in the company who you think could be a suitable candidate.

Make suggestions and give feedback on Partner A's suggestions. Try to agree on how you should recruit for this job.

Unit 2, Exercise 8   File 02

You are Jenny Mills, Personnel Assistant in the London office of Mobile plus GmbH. You are responsible for arranging and carrying out interviews for the new call centre positions. The best candidate so far for the position of team leader is Melanie Smith, who is going to call you to arrange an interview. Use your notes and this extract from your calendar to deal with the phone call and to make an appointment for an interview next week, ideally on either 7 or 8 September. (Today is 28 August.)

AUGUST / SEPTEMBER						
Monday	Tuesday	Wednesday	Thursday	Friday	Saturday	Sunday
28	29	30	31 Visit Hamburg office	1	2	3
4 10–12 Dept meeting	5	6	7 Interviews (Assess. Centre: 21st or 26th Sept?)	8	9	10

Good applicant – probable AC candidate

– give directions to office

– she should bring application form to interview

– assessment centre dates

Unit 3, Exercise 9   File 03

You are Frank/Francis Murphy and are applying for the position of bookkeeper at the German subsidiary of Greenman International Books, which is located in Stuttgart. Greenman are looking for somebody with fluent German to deal with their German clients, and although you have lived in Stuttgart for three years now, you are worried that your German won't be good enough. You are currently meeting with Stefan/Stefanie Brinkmann, the personnel officer at Greenman, to discuss the terms and conditions of the job.

Here are the things to mention at the interview:

• Flexitime? (You need to take your seven-year-old child to school each day so can't start before 9.30 am. The afternoon is no problem as your partner collects your child from school.)
• Travel expenses?
• Your German is good, but not fluent. Are lessons available?

Unit 4, Exercise 10   File 04

You are the personnel officer responsible for the recruitment section of a large HR department and are about to carry out an appraisal interview with one of your recruitment officers who has completed a year's service. You were very happy with his/her work during the six-month probationary period, but it seems something has gone wrong. You feel he/she has good potential and would like him/her to be a success.

Look at the notes you have made about some problems and prepare some questions to ask the employee during the appraisal interview. After the interview, swap roles and do the interview again.

problems over last six months
• *two periods of sickness of ten days each. What was wrong?*
• *a lot of mistakes reported*
• *complaint from a long-term employee and colleague (Becker) about long breaks from the desk, lack of attention to detail*
• *we spoke briefly three months ago (she / he was nervous and tense)*

Unit 5, Exercise 7   File 05

As members of the remuneration committee, you and two colleagues are meeting to discuss a new benefits package for your company. You have agreed to take the minutes in this second meeting.

- You personally think childcare facilities for both male and female staff are the most essential benefit to offer. (You have two children aged two and six years, and your partner is currently on maternity/paternity leave for one year.) So far only one man has taken paternity leave in your company and there are a number of female colleagues who are under extreme stress because they can't find reliable childcare they can afford.
- You don't think bonuses are a good idea; most people prefer to have a good salary and a better work/life balance.

You feel there has now been enough discussion (and you are very busy with other things at the moment), so you want to make a decision quickly! Prepare some suggestions for childcare issues to present at the meeting and try to agree with your colleagues on the next steps.

Unit 6, Exercise 13   File 06

You are a member of the works council. You have a negotiation meeting with a senior member of HR about five redundancies in the IT department. As far as you know, the five employees are being made redundant without good reason (it seems the company want to outsource the jobs to an IT consulting company) and you've heard the company isn't being very generous with its leaving package (compensation). Check your notes before going into the negotiation and try to add one or two other points to negotiate.

Points to raise at meeting
- *Over the last two years, ten key staff have been outsourced to different companies. We need some assurances this will not continue.*
- *What compensation payment is the company proposing to pay redundant employees? (Negotiate a higher one!)*
- *They say they are saving costs by outsourcing. What will the money saved be used for? Who will benefit?*
-

Partner B 1

Unit 5, Exercise 7   File 07

As members of the remuneration committee, you and two colleagues are meeting to discuss a new benefits package for your company.

Childcare issues are fine but you don't have children and would prefer to have some sort of reward incentives (profit sharing, performance-related pay, free shares in the company?) which would motivate all employees, not just the ones with children. You agree that some sort of flexible working arrangements are necessary, though; too many of your colleagues work excessive overtime and there have been one or two cases of stress-related illnesses recently.

Decide what recommendations you would like to make exactly, and be ready to present your suggestions at the meeting. Hopefully, you and your colleagues can agree on a proposal today, so you can make recommendations to management this week. (You have offered to write the email to management and you are going on a two-week holiday in three days.)

Answer key

UNIT 1

page 5

Clock-in
(suggested order)

1	i	4	d	7	f	10	j
2	a	5	g	8	h		
3	c	6	e	9	b		

1 Job description
job title
main purpose of job
reporting relationship
location of workplace
key duties/responsibilities

Person specification
desirable skills
practical requirements
previous experience
qualifications/training
skills and qualities needed for job
personal style/behaviour

page 6

2 1 Job title
2 Reports to
3 Responsible for
4 Main purpose of job
5 Key duties/responsibilities
6 Essential experience
7 Workplace location

page 7

3 1 False: The job is based in Manchester and requires a lot of travelling in Great Britain and Northern Ireland.
2 False: The training manager is responsible for two administrators, one PA and a team of trainers.
3 True
4 False: He/She reports directly to the General Manager, UK and Northern Europe.
5 True

4 1 reports to   4 carrying out
2 work; develop   5 prepare
3 implement; identify   6 involves

page 8

5 1 improve   5 develop
2 build   6 identify
3 react to   7 ensure
4 motivate

7 1 Qualifications/training
2 Previous experience
3 Skills and qualities needed for job
4 Desirable skills
5 Personal style/behaviour
6 Additional information

8 1 e   2 a   3 d   4 g   5 f   6 b   7 c

page 10

10 They mention recruiting via the intranet (in-house), using recruitment agencies that specialize in HR, and advertising in a German HR trade magazine.

page 11

1 True
2 False: The ideal candidate must have 2–5 years' *generalist* HR experience.
3 True
4 False: David is responsible for this.
5 True
6 False: The merger is not given as the reason for the job search.
7 False

11 1 to have a word about sth
2 (have been) cleared
3 generalist
4 in-house
5 merger
6 trade paper
7 to keep (sb) posted
8 disciplinary procedures

12 1 self-employed   5 re-employed
2 unemployment   6 recruited
3 employer   7 recruitment
4 employees

page 12

13 1 g   2 e   3 f   4 b   5 a   6 c   7 d

UNIT 2

page 14

Clock-in
(suggested answers with comments)
1 Agree: An applicant should be able to summarize his/her background in a concise and clear way in a maximum of two pages.
2 Agree and disagree: A photo is still expected in German-speaking countries but it is not considered appropriate in the UK or the US, as it is felt that how a person looks should not influence a decision to interview or not.
3 Agree: In these days of age discrimination, it is no longer necessary to put the date of birth on a CV. It is optional. An HR person can get a very good idea of an applicant's age by looking at the details of their education and experience. (See also the clock-out in this unit.)
4 Agree: In the UK or US interviewers take names and addresses of referees, or applicants put the details on their CV and a direct application for a reference by letter or phone is made by the recruitment people. Jobs are offered 'subject to satisfactory reference' until the references are received.

5 Disagree: In the UK this would be frowned on – only a two-page CV and a covering letter or email should be sent with an application. Any other documents will be asked for if/when required.

6 Agree: This is good HR practice. The applicant is then fully informed before the interview and better prepared for the questions that will be asked. Additionally, applicants have a chance to decide before an interview if they are suitable for or really interested in the position.

7 Agree: This is sound advice for applicants as most HR people wouldn't expect interviewees to wear jeans to an interview, unless they are a particularly relaxed media company/advertising agency for example.

8 Disagree: This is private information and does not make a woman more or less suitable for the job. It is also against sex discrimination laws.

1 (suggested answer)
Jobs in the travel business always attract applicants, especially when concessionary travel is mentioned. The style of the ad is also informal and has a challenging feel to it.

2   1 e   2 h   3 c   4 g   5 d   6 f   7 b   8 a

page 15

3   1 The hours of work will vary. You'll be working on a shift basis, which includes weekends and bank holidays.
   2 The main responsibilities are dealing with reservations and customer travel needs, promoting Virgin's range of services and general customer service.
   3 You will handle around 100 calls a day.
   4 The job is located in Crawley.
   5 It will consist of a group interview for 90 minutes, followed by a series of exercises and then an individual interview with two assessors. You will be notified of the results in writing.
   6 In addition to the salary, you'll receive a shift allowance and a salary increase upon completion of the six-month probationary period.
   7 A generous holiday entitlement, a pension, life assurance, Virgin discounts and cheaper travel.
   8 No, the benefits are discretionary, which means the employer will decide who gets what.

page 16

4 personal profile = outstanding qualities, a brief summary of your work experience and abilities
training = relevant courses attended, qualifications or certificates from on-the-job training
key skills = achievements/skills in career, language skills
career history = duties in previous jobs, previous employers, dates of previous employment
personal details = name and address, nationality, full contact details, marital status, specializations/publications, professional qualification or title (eg BSc, PhD)
education = school and university details, main exams or degree

Not all CVs have the same layout, but as a general rule the following might be a logical order:
1 personal details
2 personal profile
3 career history (last job first)
4 key skills
5 education
6 training

5   1 g   2 f   3 d   4 b   5 a   6 j   7 e
    8 c   9 i   10 h

page 17

6   1 False: She applied for a position as Call Centre *Team Leader*.
   2 True
   3 False: The *initial interview* will take place within two weeks.
   4 True
   5 False: Details will be sent in advanced to the applicants who are selected.
   6 True
   7 False: She has to call the London office to arrange the interview.

page 18

7 Correct order: c – a – f – e – d – b

page 19

9   1 has resigned/handed in her notice
   2 take on/hire; notice/resignation
   3 lay off
   4 made redundant/let go
   5 dismissed/sacked/fired
   6 offered early retirement

10 (suggested answer)
    1 f   2 b   3 g   4 a   5 c   6 d   7 h   8 e

page 20

11 She asks open questions which require full (and not just yes and no) answers.

page 21

12   1 b   2 a   3 a   4 a   5 b   6 a   7 a

13 (suggested answers)
    1 Melanie Smith
    2 team leader, London call centre
    3 promoted to team leader 2 years ago
    4 6 years' experience in customer service
    5 responsible for 10 staff in call centre
    6 direct responsibility for difficult customers
    7 in constant communication with own staff, regular weekly meetings, call centre staff move around teams to gain experience
    8 enjoys customer contact and solving problems
    9 company is relocating, doesn't wish to move (children at school/partner working in the same area)
    10 seem excellent, she is used to a well structured call centre, and relationships with customers are given top priority.

page 22

14 (suggested answers)
1   Could you tell me about your relationship with your present supervisor?/How do you get on with ...?
2   Could you outline one or two staff problems you have had and how you dealt with them?
3   Could you give some examples of how you handle customers well?
4   What shift hours do you normally work?
5   Could you give me some details of decisions you have had to make on your own initiative?
6   How well do you work under pressure? Could you give some examples?

16 1   applicants
2   application
3   applicable
4   selective
5   selection
6   assessment
7   assess

UNIT 3

page 24

Clock-in
1c   sex discrimination
2h   contract of employment
3e   equal pay
4d   maternity leave
5b   workplace injuries
6a   short-time working
7g   disciplinary and grievance procedure
8f   work-related stress

page 25

1 1   False: The company doesn't have flexitime yet.
2   True (plus payment under the 'Permanent Health Insurance Scheme' after that)
3   True
4   False: She wrote the names of the referees on the application form.
5   False: She has told them already.
6   False: She'll receive it in the next couple of days.

page 26

2 **Across**
6   permanent
7   procedures
8   in lieu
9   clear

Down
1   referees
2   honour
3   contract
4   offer
5   reference

3 **Working time**
shift work
part-time employment
core time
six-day week
flexitime

Employment status
trial period
fixed-term contract
temporary employment
probationary period

Holidays
annual leave
sick leave
public holiday
vacation (US)
holiday entitlement

Leaving employment
notice period
resignation
dismissal
redundancy

4 1   flexible
2   flextime (or flexitime)
3   flexibility
4   inflexible

page 27

5 1 e   2 c   3 h   4 g   5 j   6 d   7 a   8 i   9 f   10 b

page 28

6 1   can be found
2   may be required
3   are expected
4   will be discussed, notified in writing
5   are entitled to
6   payable monthly in arrears
7   are asked; notify
8   subject to disciplinary action

7   Offer letter
d – c – i – a – f

Rejection letter
g – b – h – j – e

See model offer and rejection letters on pages 75–76.

page 29

8 1 c   2 e   3 h   4 a   5 d   6 f   7 b   8 g

page 30

10 1   occur
2   conditions
3   safety
4   entitled
5   entitlement
6   breaking
7   disciplinary
8   representative
9   policy
10   behaviour

page 31

11 (suggested answers)
1   More people are taking time off work due to sickness.
2   Some companies send staff to their own (in-house) company doctor.
3   Women are going to court because they feel they are treated unfairly just because they are women.
4   The Japanese problem of death from overwork continues to grow in Japan.
5   Using the Internet for accessing pornographic or other non-business sites can lead to dismissal, but in this case the employer has allowed the staff responsible to resign.
6   More and more companies are encouraging staff to look after their health.

7 Not allowing employees to smoke at work has reduced the number of heart attacks in the US.

8 Some industrial companies are discussing ways to reduce noise levels in the workplace to prevent health problems.

page 32

13 1 c   2 b   3 a   4 b   5 c   6 c   7 a   8 a
9 c   10 a

Clock-out

a 7.5 million working days are lost each year in the UK due to accidents in the workplace.

b 249 people died in accidents at work during 2001 and 2002.

c 127,000 accidents required staff to be off work for over three days.

d 563,000 people suffered from mental health problems last year.

UNIT 4

page 33

Clock-in

The statements refer to the following types of HR development.

1 long-term individual development
2 appraisal (performance management)
3 induction programme
4 equal opportunity policies

1 1 flexible working practices
2 secondment
3 long-term individual development
4 appraisal
5 equal opportunity policies
6 team development
7 mentoring
8 induction programme

page 34

2 1 d   2 a   3 c   4 b

page 35

3 1 recommend
2 high time; essential
3 need to; we should
4 I propose
5 proposal

4 (suggested answers)

1 Clearly the company has a problem with equal pay. As soon as they clarify the situation, they should ensure that there aren't any other discrepancies like this. They should also check that their equal opportunity policies generally are in place.

2 They should consider the advantages of introducing some flexible working practices into the company before too many other staff leave. Introducing some sort of flexitime system and then looking closely at their parental policies would be good places to start.

5 Other reasons for appraisal: rewarding staff for good performance (salary review), succession planning (the process of planning promotions and managerial positions for the future), encouraging better communication and formal assessment of unsatisfactory performance

page 36

6 This is a normal annual appraisal interview to discuss progress in the past year and to resolve any problems.

page 37

7 1 to detail
2 relationships
3 delegate
4 decrease
5 skills
6 long-term sickness
7 overtime
8 communicate
9 cultural
10 production director
11 leadership
12 training manager

(suggested answers)

13 I must maintain better communication with Peter (weekly meetings).

14 Peter will discuss how to increase output in the short term with his team.

page 38

8 1 b   2 f   3 d   4 e   5 a   6 c

9 1 How do you see the relationship with your team?
2 ... you were actually 25 per cent down for six months ...
3 Why didn't you raise this issue (at the regular team meeting)?
4 I'm concerned you didn't feel able to discuss it with me.
5 The results are not very impressive, Peter.
6 You need to think about delegating more ...
7 I think you and I need to improve our communication ...
8 Finally, on a personal note, Peter, how is your wife settling in?

page 39

11 1 Leadership and team building
2 Managing your time
3 Assertive leadership skills
4 Balancing priorities and managing projects

12 1 competent leader
2 peer group
3 to take control
4 to get results
5 to set priorities
6 to complete tasks
7 to fulfil targets
8 to handle people

page 40

14 1 Equal
2 equally
3 inequality
4 appraisal
5 appraisers; appraisees

15 These statements have been taken from various job advertisements in newspapers and trade magazines. In the UK most job advertisements contain this type of statement to create a good impression and to show that the companies support diversity. It is considered good employment practice and gives an idea of the atmosphere inside a company.

UNIT 5

page 42

Clock-in
See exercise 4 for ideas.

1 Benefits mentioned are:
- flexible working hours
- childcare and eldercare
- profit-sharing bonuses

page 43

2 1 Heike called the meeting to discuss their benefits package.
2 Paola felt they needed to introduce more flexibility for staff.
3 Sven was in favour of giving employees greater freedom to have a good work/life balance.
4 He was keen to encourage female staff back to work.
5 Sven will prepare a proposal to submit at the next regular meeting.
6 Heike asked Paola to prepare a summary of benefits and costs.
7 Paola has already talked to colleagues in other offices about flexitime initiatives.
8 Heike is going to inform Paola and Sven about the new profit-sharing bonus at their next meeting.

3 1 I have your input
2 Could you please
3 do you mean
4 you know
5 definitely in favour
6 I think we should also
7 fine

page 44

4 1 f   2 h   3 k   4 b   5 j   6 c

7 l   8 a   9 d   10 g   11 i   12 e

page 45

5 1 contributory
2 creche
3 pension
4 share
5 cafeteria
6 merit
7 relocation
8 counselling

The hidden word is: benefits.

6 1 benefit
2 benefits
3 beneficiary
4 reviewed
5 reviews

page 46

8 1 Best wishes
2 initial
3 recommend
4 information
5 of
6 was
7 offer
8 workforce

The order of sentences: e – c – f – b – d – a.

(model answer in email layout)

> Dear Board Members
>
> At a meeting *of* the Remuneration Committee last week, the question of a new benefits package was raised. We would like to *recommend* that the attached proposals be introduced over the next two years.
>
> We feel this would *offer* the staff more flexible working arrangements, while benefiting the company in terms of a happy and contented *workforce*. We appreciate that it will be necessary to hold a detailed meeting about this, but we look forward to hearing your *initial* comments.
>
> If you require any further *information*, please let us know.
>
> *Best wishes*
> Remuneration Committee

9

upward	downward
an increase	a drop
a raise	less
to rise	to slash

page 47

10 1 The Board *has already agreed 5%* [not 5.5%] from 1 October.
2 I told Heike there are *one or two people* [not six] who should get more than 5% (those who relocated from *New York* and *London* [not Canada]).
3 Correct
4 Correct
5 Performance reviews will take place *in November and early December* [not in the new year].
6 They are *only thinking about* introducing flexible working.
7 Correct
8 Correct
9 Correct

page 48

11 1 five thousand euros
2 sixty thousand pounds per annum
3 fifty million, two hundred and thirty nine thousand, one hundred and fifty dollars
4 seventy billion euros
5 a/one hundred and ten million dollars
6 a/one hundred and fifty pounds per hour

12 1 e   2 d   3 a   4 c   5 b   6 f

UNIT 6

page 50

Clock-in

1 Correct
2 Correct
3 False: The largest union in Germany is Ver.di.
4 Correct
5 Correct
6 False: A union's main responsibility is to look after its *members'* interests.
7 Correct
8 False: The strike was over planned pension reforms.

1 1 campaigning
2 a global initiative
3 collective agreement
4 a counter-offer

page 51

2 1 g put forward a counter-offer
2 b negotiate pay and conditions
3 a enforce a closed shop
4 c take industrial action
5 d look after employees' interests
6 f discuss a collective agreement
7 e be involved in wage negotiations

page 52

3 Statement b best describes the situation.

4 1 *behind:* The union wants the same increase as the white-collar workers.
2 *counter-:* He said that they had a 3% review a year ago, sales were down and there might have to be redundancies in Amsterdam if things don't improve.
3 *fail; agreement:* The union felt 3% was too low. They want 5% or they will take industrial action.
4 *freeze:* The company lost a big contract and there was also a recession.
5 *rumours:* The rumours are that work will be transferred to Poland due to an economic downturn in the industry.
5 *tactics:* The last thing they want is a strike and they cannot pay 5%, so a good outcome has to be achieved when they meet the union again.

page 53

5 1 b 2 a 3 b 4 a 5 b 6 a

6 (suggested order)
1 Prepare your arguments.
2 Be flexible and prepared to compromise.
3 Always remember your aims.
4 Use simple and clear language.
5 Always listen carefully to the other person.
6 Build rapport and be courteous.
7 Be positive – highlight the 'common ground'.
8 Be constructive and avoid conflict.
9 Use persuasion – not threats.
10 When agreement is reached, summarize clearly and close the deal.

page 54

7 building rapport   4, 7
establishing objectives and aims   9, 10
bargaining   2, 6
addressing conflict   3, 5
concluding   1, 8

8 Sentences in dialogue: 3, 4, 6, 7, 8, 9 and 10

page 55

9 1 met
2 are receiving
3 have been
4 transferring
5 gave
6 was not
7 is not
8 accepted

page 56

10 (suggested answers)
1 Unless our members get a 5% increase in pay, they will take industrial action.
2 Provided that there is an increase in sales, we can offer a further 2% pay rise
3 If we don't give a further increase in pay, there will be no job losses in Amsterdam.
4 There will be no industrial action on condition that there is another review in nine months.
5 If productivity increased, we could pay a bonus at the end of the year.
6 We'll lose business to our competitors unless we open on Sundays from 10–4 pm.
7 Provided customer service doesn't suffer, we can introduce flexible working hours.

page 57

12 1 negotiator
2 negotiable
3 negotiation
4 consultant
5 consultative
6 Consultation

pages 58–59

Test yourself!

Across		Down	
1	rejection	1	remuneration
5	relocate	2	council
9	induction	3	harassment
11	unemployed	4	generalist
15	perks	6	conflict
19	open	7	flexitime
20	appraisal	8	notice
22	reference	10	description
23	rise	12	overtime
25	balance	13	disciplinary
27	equal pay	14	allowance
28	diversity	16	shop floor
29	maternity	17	discrimination
30	probationary	18	candidate
		21	grievance
		24	closed
		26	employment

A–Z word list

A

ability [ə'bɪləti]	Fähigkeit, Können	
access ['ækses]	Zugang	
to **accompany** [ə'kʌmpəni]	begleiten	
accord, of one's own ~	auf eigenen Wunsch	
[ɒn wʌnz 'əʊn ə,kɔːd]		
according to [ə'kɔːdɪŋ tə]	laut, nach	
account, to take into ~	berücksichtigen	
[,teɪk ɪntu ə'kaʊnt]		
accuracy ['ækjərəsi]	Genauigkeit	
to **achieve** [ə'tʃiːv]	erreichen, erzielen	
acknowledgement	Bestätigung	
[ək'nɒlɪdʒmənt]		
action, to take positive ~	aktive Schritte einleiten, Schritte	
[teɪk ,pɒzətɪv 'ækʃn]	unternehmen	
to **adjust** [ə'dʒʌst]	anpassen	
administrator [əd'mɪnɪstreɪtə]	(Personal-)Sachbearbeiter	
to **advertise** ['ædvətaɪz]	inserieren, eine Stellenanzeige	
	aufgeben	
to **afford** [ə'fɔːd]	(es) sich leisten (können)	
to **agree** [ə'griː]	festlegen, vereinbaren	
to **amend** [ə'mend]	(ab)ändern	
ankle ['æŋkl]	Fußgelenk, Knöchel	
annual ['ænjuəl]	jährlich	
annual leave [,ænjuəl 'liːv]	Jahresurlaub	
anxiety [æŋ'zaɪəti]	Angst(zustand)	
anxious ['æŋkʃəs]	besorgt, beunruhigt	
applicant ['æplɪkənt]	Bewerber/in	
application [,æplɪ'keɪʃn]	Bewerbung	
appraisal interview	Bewertungsgespräch	
[ə,preɪzl 'ɪntəvjuː]		
appraisal [ə'preɪzl]	Bewertung	
appraisee [əpreɪ'ziː]	Beurteilte/r	
appraiser [ə'preɪzə]	Beurteiler/in	
to **appreciate** [ə'priːʃieɪt]	dankbar sein für, schätzen	
appropriate [ə'prəʊpriət]	angemessen, passend	
approval [ə'pruːvl]	Zustimmung, Genehmigung	
argumentative [,ɑːgju'mentətɪv]	streitsüchtig	
arrears, in ~ [ɪn ə'rɪəz]	rückwirkend	
assertive [ə'sɜːtɪv]	energisch	
to **assess** [ə'ses]	beurteilen, begutachten	
assurances [ə'ʃʊərənsɪz]	Zusicherung, Zusagen	
to **attend** [ə'tend]	teilnehmen (an)	
attitude ['ætɪtjuːd]	Einstellung, Haltung	
to **avert** [ə'vɜːt]	abwenden	
awareness [ə'weənəs]	Bewusstsein	

B

bank holiday [,bæŋk 'hɒlədeɪ]	öffentlicher Feiertag
bankruptcy ['bæŋkrʌpsi]	Bankrott, Konkurs
to **bar sb from sth** ['bɑː frəm]	jdn von etw ausschließen
to **bargain** ['bɑːgɪn]	verhandeln
based in ['beɪst ɪn]	der Arbeitsort ist
to **be inclined to** [bi ɪn'klaɪnd tə]	dazu neigen
behalf, on ~ of [ɒn bɪ'hɑːf əv]	im Namen von
behind, to be ~ sth [bi bɪ'haɪnd]	dahinterstecken
behind, to get ~ [,get bɪ'haɪnd]	im Rückstand sein
benefits package	Vergünstigungen, Zusatz-
['benɪfɪts pækɪdʒ]	leistungen
blue-collar workers	(Fabrik-)Arbeiter
[,bluː 'kɒlə wɜːkəz]	
board (of directors)	Aufsichtsrat, (Firmen-)Vorstand
[,bɔːd əv də'rektəz]	
bonus ['bəʊnəs]	Zulage, Prämie, Bonus
bottom line [,bɒtəm 'laɪn]	Endergebnis
branch manager	Filialleiter/in
['brɑːntʃ mænɪdʒə]	
brief [briːf]	kurz
bright [braɪt]	leuchtend, hell

building society ['bɪldɪŋ səsaɪəti]	Bausparkasse
bullying ['bʊliɪŋ]	Mobbing

C

cards on the table, to put ~	die Karten auf den Tisch legen
[pʊt ,kɑːdz ɒn ðə 'teɪbl]	
to **carry out** [,kæri 'aʊt]	durchführen
chain [tʃeɪn]	(Handels-)Kette
challenging ['tʃælɪndʒɪŋ]	(heraus)fordernd
childcare ['tʃaɪldkeə]	Kinderbetreuung
to **clarify** ['klærəfaɪ]	(näher) erläutern, klären
to **clear sth with sb** [klɪə wɪð]	mit jdm (ab)klären
client ['klaɪənt]	Kunde/Kundin
closure ['kləʊʒə]	Schließung
collective agreement	Tarifvereinbarung, Manteltarif
[kə,lektɪv ə'griːmənt]	
collective bargaining	Tarifverhandlung, -abkommen
[kə,lektɪv 'bɑːgənɪŋ]	
commencing salary	Anfangsgehalt
[kə,mensɪŋ 'sæləri]	
committed to [kə'mɪtɪd tə]	engagiert für
compensation [,kɒmpən'seɪʃn]	Entschädigung, Abfindung
competency ['kɒmpɪtənsi]	Kompetenz, Fähigkeit
competent ['kɒmpɪtənt]	kompetent, fähig
competitor ['kɒmpetɪtə(r)]	Konkurrent/in, Konkurrenz
complaint [kəm'pleɪnt]	Beanstandung, Reklamation
complimentary close	Schlussformel, Gruß(formel)
[,kɒmplɪ,mentri 'kləʊz]	
concerned, as far as X is ~	was X betrifft
[əz ,fɑːr əz eks ɪz kən'sɜːnd]	
concerned, to be ~ [bi kən'sɜːnd]	besorgt sein
concessionary travel	Ermäßigungen auf Reisen
[kən,seʃənəri 'trævl]	
to **conduct (an interview)**	(ein Vorstellungsgespräch)
[kən'dʌkt]	(durch)führen
confidence, in the strictest ~	streng vertraulich
['kɒnfɪdəns]	
conflict, open ~ [,əʊpən 'kɒnflɪkt]	offener Konflikt
to **consider** [kən'sɪdə]	prüfen
to **consist of** [kən'sɪst əv]	bestehen aus, sich zusammen-
	setzen aus
consistent [kən'sɪstənt]	einheitlich, gleichbleibend,
	aufeinander abgestimmt
to **consult** [kən'sʌlt]	(sich) beraten
consultancy [kən'sʌltənsi]	Beratungsbüro
to **contain** [kən'teɪn]	unter Kontrolle bringen
to **contribute** [kən'trɪbjuːt]	beitragen
control, to take ~ [teɪk kən'trəʊl]	die Kontrolle haben/behalten
convenient [kən'viːniənt]	passend, günstig
to **cope** [kəʊp]	(damit) zurechtkommen, fertig-
	werden
core time ['kɔː taɪm]	Kernzeit
corporate identity (CI)	Firmenphilosophie, Corporate
[,kɔːpərət aɪ'dentəti]	Identity
counselling ['kaʊnsəlɪŋ]	Beratung
counter-argument	Gegenargument
[,kaʊntər 'ɑːgjumənt]	
counter-offer ['kaʊntə ɒfə]	Gegenangebot
courteous ['kɜːtiəs]	höflich
crèche [kreʃ]	(Kinder-)Krippe, Kinderhort
creed [kriːd]	Glaube(nsbekenntnis)
currently ['kʌrəntli]	momentan, zurzeit
curriculum vitae	Lebenslauf
[kə,rɪkjələm 'viːtaɪ]	

D

deadline, to meet a ~	einen Termin einhalten
[miːt ə 'dedlaɪn]	
decrease ['diːkriːs]	Rückgang

degree [dɪˈgriː] — (akademischer) Abschluss
dependant [dɪˈpendənt] — Angehörige/r
desirable skill [dɪˈzaɪərəbl skɪl] — wünschenswerte Fähigkeit/ Fertigkeit
to **detail** [ˈdiːteɪl] — detailliert aufführen
to **determine** [dɪˈtɜːmɪn] — bestimmen
directive [dəˈrektɪv] — Anordnung, Direktive
disability [ˌdɪsəˈbɪləti] — Behinderung
disciplinary action [ˌdɪsəplɪnəri ˈækʃn] — Disziplinarverfahren
disciplinary procedures [ˌdɪsəplɪnəri prəˈsiːdʒəz] — Disziplinarmaßnahmen
discount scheme [dɪˈskaʊnt skiːm] — Rabattsystem
discretionary benefit [dɪˌskreʃənəri ˈbenɪfɪt] — zusätzliche Leistung nach Ermessen
to **discriminate against** [dɪˈskrɪmɪneɪt əgenst] — diskriminieren
to **dismiss** [dɪsˈmɪs] — entlassen
dismissal [dɪsˈmɪsl] — Entlassung, Freisetzung
to **downsize** [ˈdaʊnsaɪz] — (sich) verkleinern, Stellen abbauen
draft agenda [drɑːft əˈdʒendə] — Entwurf der Tagesordnung
drop, to take a ~ in salary [taɪk ə drɒp ɪn ˈsæləri] — Lohneinbußen hinnehmen
due to [ˈdjuː tə] — wegen, aufgrund von
duties [ˈdjuːtiz] — Aufgaben, Pflichten

E
early retirement [ˌɜːli rɪˈtaɪəmənt] — vorzeitiger Ruhestand, Vorruhestand
economic downturn [ˌiːkəˌnɒmɪk ˈdaʊntɜːn] — Wirtschaftsflaute, Rezession
effort, in an ~ to [ɪn ən ˈefət tə] — im Bestreben zu
eldercare [ˈeldəkeə] — Altenpflege
to **employ** [ɪmˈplɔɪ] — an-, einstellen, beschäftigen
employ, in our own ~ [ɪmˈplɔɪ] — bei uns beschäftigt
employee [ɪmˈplɔɪiː] — Arbeitnehmer/in, Angestellte/r
employer [ɪmˈplɔɪə] — Arbeitgeber/in
employment legislation [ɪmˌplɔɪmənt ˌledʒɪsˈleɪʃn] — Arbeitsgesetze
to **empower** [ɪmˈpaʊə] — befähigen, etw zu tun
to **enable** [ɪˈneɪbl] — ermöglichen
to **enclose** [ɪnˈkləʊz] — beilegen, beifügen
to **encourage** [ɪnˈkʌrɪdʒ] — fördern, unterstützen
to **enforce** [ɪnˈfɔːs] — erzwingen
to **engage** [ɪnˈgeɪdʒ] — einstellen
to **enhance** [ɪnˈhɑːns] — erhöhen, steigern, verbessern
to **enlarge on sth** [ɪnˈlɑːdʒ ɒn] — etw genauer beschreiben
to **ensure** [ɪnˈʃʊə(r)] — gewährleisten
entitled, to be ~ to [bi ɪnˈtaɪtld tə] — Anspruch haben auf
entitlement [ɪnˈtaɪtlmənt] — Anspruch
equal opportunity policy [ˌiːkwəl ɒpəˌtjuːnəti ˈpɒləsi] — Chancengleichheit
equal pay [ˌiːkwəl ˈpeɪ] — gleiche Bezahlung
essential [ɪˈsenʃl] — wesentlich, notwendig
ethnic origin [ˌeθnɪk ˈɒrɪdʒɪn] — ethnische Herkunft
evaluation [ɪˌvæljuˈeɪʃn] — (Ein-)Schätzung, Bewertung
event, in the ~ of [ɪn ði ɪˈvent əv] — im Falle von
experience [ɪkˈspɪəriəns] — (Berufs-)Erfahrung
exposure to [ɪkˈspəʊʒə] — etw/jdm ausgesetzt sein
extent, to a certain ~ [tu ə ˌsɜːtn ɪkˈstent] — in gewissem Maße, bis zu einem bestimmten Punkt

F
failure to do so [ˈfeɪljə] — bei Nichteinhaltung
to **familiarize** [fəˈmɪliəraɪz] — vertraut machen
field of work [fiːld əv ˈwɜːk] — Arbeitsgebiet, -bereich
to **fill sb in on sth** [fɪl ɪn ɒn] — jdn über etw unterrichten
to **finalize** [ˈfaɪnəlaɪz] — endgültig festlegen
to **fire** (US) [ˈfaɪə] — feuern, hinauswerfen
fire drill [ˈfaɪə drɪl] — Probealarm
first aider [ˌfɜːst ˈeɪdə] — erste Hilfe
fixed-term contract [ˌfɪkst tɜːm ˈkɒntrækt] — befristeter Arbeitsvertrag

flexitime [ˈfleksitaɪm] — Gleitzeit
fork lift truck [ˌfɔːklɪft ˈtrʌk] — Gabelstapler
formality [fɔːˈmæləti] — Förmlichkeit
frank, to be ~ [bi ˈfræŋk] — offen gesagt
to **freeze salaries** [friːz ˈsæləriz] — Gehälter einfrieren
fringe benefits [ˈfrɪndʒ benɪfɪts] — zusätzliche Sozialleistungen, Zusatzleistungen

G
gender [ˈdʒendə] — Geschlecht
generalist [ˈdʒenrəlɪst] — als Generalist
grateful [ˈgreɪtfl] — dankbar
grievance procedure [ˌgriːvəns prəˈsiːdʒə] — innerbetriebliches Beschwerdeverfahren

H
to **hand in one's notice** [ˌhænd ɪn ˈnəʊtɪs] — kündigen (durch den Arbeitnehmer/Angestellten)
hands-on work [ˌhændz ɒn ˈwɜːk] — praktische Arbeit
harassment [ˈhærəsmənt] — Belästigung
hard hat [ˌhɑːd ˈhæt] — Schutzhelm
to **head** [hed] — (an)führen, leiten
high time [ˌhaɪ ˈtaɪm] — höchste Zeit
to **hire** (US) [ˈhaɪə] — ein-, anstellen
to **hire a replacement** [ˌhaɪər ə rɪˈpleɪsmənt] — einen Mitarbeiter ersetzen/eine Arbeitsstelle neu besetzen
to **hold pending** [ˈhəʊld ˌpendɪŋ] — vorerst behalten bis …
to **honour** [ˈɒnə] — anerkennen
horizon, on the ~ [ɒn ðə həˈraɪzn] — in Sicht
hot under the collar [ˌhɒt ʌndə ðə ˈkɒlə] — wütend

I
to **implement** [ˈɪmplɪment] — umsetzen, einführen
incentive [ɪnˈsentɪv] — Anreiz
individual development [ˌɪndɪˌvɪdʒuəl dɪˈveləpmənt] — individuelle Entwicklung
induction [ɪnˈdʌkʃn] — Arbeitseinführung
industrial action [ɪnˌdʌstriəl ˈækʃn] — Arbeitskampf(maßnahmen), Ausstand
initiative, to work on one's own ~ [wɜːk ɒn wʌnz əʊn ɪˈnɪʃətɪv] — eigenverantwortlich arbeiten
to **instruct** [ɪnˈstrʌkt] — anweisen, beauftragen
internal staff [ɪnˈtɜːnl stɑːf] — (bereits) vorhandene Mitarbeiter
interpersonal skills [ˌɪntəˈpɜːsənl skɪlz] — der Umgang mit anderen Menschen
interview, (job) ~ [ˈɪntəvjuː] — Ein-, Vorstellungsgespräch
intimidation [ɪnˌtɪmɪˈdeɪʃn] — Einschüchterung
to **involve** [ɪnˈvɒlv] — einschließen, beinhalten
to **issue sb with sth** [ˈɪʃuː] — etw an jdn ausgeben
issues [ˈɪʃuːz] — Fragen, Angelegenheiten

JK
job advert(isement) [dʒɒb ˈædvɜːt, ədˈvɜːtɪsmənt] — Stellenanzeige
job description [dʒɒb dɪˈskrɪpʃn] — Stellenbeschreibung
job seeker [ˈdʒɒb siːkə] — Arbeitssuchende/r
job title [ˈdʒɒb taɪtl] — Berufsbezeichnung
job-sharing [ˈdʒɒb ʃeərɪŋ] — Arbeitsplatzteilung
to **keep sb posted** [kiːp ˈpəʊstɪd] — jdn auf dem Laufenden halten

L
labor union (US) [ˈleɪbə juːniən] — Gewerkschaft
labour market [ˈleɪbə mɑːkɪt] — Arbeitsmarkt
law [lɔː] — Recht, Gesetz
to **lay off** [ˌleɪ ˈɒf] — (zeitweilig) entlassen
leaving package [ˈliːvɪŋ pækɪdʒ] — Abfindungsregelung
to **let go** [ˌlet ˈgəʊ] — gehen lassen
liaison [liˈeɪzn] — Zusammenarbeit
life assurance [ˈlaɪf əʃʊərəns] — Lebensversicherung
line manager [laɪn ˈmænɪdʒə] — Produktmanager/in
load [ləʊd] — Last
long-term [ˌlɒŋˈtɜːm] — langfristig
to **look forward to** [ˌlʊk ˈfɔːwəd tə] — sich freuen auf
to **look into sth** [ˌlʊk ˈɪntə] — etw prüfen

M

to **maintain** [meɪn'teɪn]	bewahren, aufrechterhalten, pflegen	
managerial [ˌmænə'dʒɪərɪəl]	Management-, Führungs-	
marital status [ˌmærɪtl 'steɪtəs]	Familienstand	
maternity leave [mə'tɜːnəti liːv]	Mutterschutz, Elternzeit (für die Mutter)	
measure ['meʒə(r)]	Maßnahme	
to **mention** ['menʃn]	erwähnen	
mentoring ['mentɔːrɪŋ]	Mentorenbetreuung	
merger ['mɜːdʒə]	Fusion	
merit, on a ~ basis [ɒn ə 'merɪt beɪsɪs]	leistungsorientiert, leistungsbezogen	
mileage allowance [ˌmaɪlɪdʒ ə'laʊəns]	Kilometergeld	
monetary terms ['mʌnɪtri tɜːmz]	finanzielle Hinsicht	
to **monitor** ['mɒnɪtə(r)]	kontrollieren	
moving expenses [ˌmuːvɪŋ ɪk'spensɪz]	Umzugskosten	
to **muddle through** [ˌmʌdl 'θruː]	sich durchwursteln	

N

to **negotiate** [nɪ'gəʊʃieɪt]	ver-, aushandeln
non-contributory [ˌnɒn kən'trɪbjətri]	beitragsfrei
notice ['nəʊtɪs]	Kündigung(sfrist)
to **notify** ['nəʊtɪfaɪ]	benachrichtigen

O

to **obtain** [əb'teɪn]	erhalten
to **occur** [ə'kɜː]	vorkommen
odds, the ~ [ðɪ 'ɒdz]	die Chancen, Aussichten
on-going ['ɒn gəʊɪŋ]	laufend
outlook ['aʊtlʊk]	Aussichten, Ausblick
to **outsource** ['aʊtsɔːs]	auslagern, outsourcen
outstanding [aʊt'stændɪŋ]	hervorragend
overdue [ˌəʊvə'djuː]	überfällig
overtime ['əʊvətaɪm]	Überstunden

P

particular [pə'tɪkjələ]	besondere(r,s), speziell
paternity leave [pə'tɜːnəti liːv]	Elternzeit (für den Vater)
pay deal ['peɪ diːl]	Lohnabschluss
payable ['peɪəbl]	zahlbar, fällig
peer group ['pɪə gruːp]	Gleichrangige, (direkte) Kollegen
pension ['penʃn]	Rente, Pension
performance-related pay [pə'fɔːməns rɪleɪtɪd peɪ]	Leistungslohn, leistungsgerechte Zahlung
perk [pɜːk]	betriebliche/freiwillige Sozialleistung
person specification [ˌpɜːsn ˌspesɪfɪ'keɪʃn]	Anforderungsprofil
personal assistant [ˌpɜːsənl ə'sɪstənt]	(persönliche/r) Assistent/in
personnel [ˌpɜːsə'nel]	Personal, Mitarbeiter
personnel officer [ˌpɜːsə'nel ɒfɪsə]	Mitarbeiter/in in der Personalabteilung
to **persuade** [pə'sweɪd]	überzeugen, überreden
to **picket** ['pɪkɪt]	Streikposten einsetzen
to **place** [pleɪs]	platzieren, aufgeben
plant [plɑːnt]	Werk, Betrieb
point, to have a ~ [həv ə 'pɔɪnt]	Recht haben, etw dran sein
policy ['pɒləsi]	(Firmen-)Politik
to **postpone** [pə'spəʊn]	verschieben
previous ['priːvɪəs]	bisherig, vorherig
priorities, to set ~ [set praɪ'ɒrɪtiz]	Prioritäten setzen
to **prioritize** [praɪ'ɒrətaɪz]	Prioritäten setzen
probationary period [prə,beɪʃnri 'pɪərɪəd]	Probezeit
productivity bonus [ˌprɒdʌk'tɪvəti bəʊnəs]	Leistungszulage
profit-sharing ['prɒfɪt ʃeərɪŋ]	Gewinnbeteiligung
promotion [prə'məʊʃn]	Beförderung
protective clothing [prə,tektɪv 'kləʊðɪŋ]	Schutzkleidung
provision [prə'vɪʒn]	Vorkehrung, Bestimmung

publications [ˌpʌblɪ'keɪʃnz]	Veröffentlichungen
purpose of ['pɜːpəs əv]	Zweck
to **pursue** [pə'sjuː]	verfolgen, nachgehen

R

raise (US) [reɪz]	(Gehalts-)Erhöhung
to **raise** [reɪz]	anschneiden
range of ['reɪndʒ əv]	Reihe von
rapport [ræ'pɔː]	(enges) Verhältnis
rate of pay [ˌreɪt əv 'peɪ]	Entgelt, Bezahlung
to **reach agreement** [riːtʃ ə'griːmənt]	sich einigen
to **react to** [ri'ækt tə]	reagieren auf
to **record** [rɪ'kɔːd]	aufzeichnen, festhalten
recruitment assessor [rɪ,kruːtmənt ə'sesə]	Beobachter (während eines Auswahlprozesses/AC)
recruitment officer [rɪ'kruːtmənt ɒfɪsə]	Einstellungssachbearbeiter/in
recruitment [rɪ'kruːtmənt]	Einstellung (von Arbeitskräften), Personalbeschaffung
redundancy [rɪ'dʌndənsi]	Entlassung, Freisetzung
redundant, to make ~ [ˌmeɪk rɪ'dʌndənt]	entlassen, freisetzen
referee [ˌrefə'riː]	Referenzgeber/in, Zeugnisaussteller/in
reference ['refərəns]	Referenz, (Arbeits-)Zeugnis
references, to take up ~ [teɪk ˌʌp 'refərənsɪz]	Referenzen einholen
to **refuse to** [rɪ'fjuːz tə]	ablehnen, sich weigern
regardless of [rɪ'gɑːdləs əv]	ungeachtet
to **regret** [rɪ'gret]	bedauern
to **reimburse sb for sth** [ˌriːɪm'bɜːs]	jdn für etw entschädigen
to **reject** [rɪ'dʒekt]	ablehnen
rejection (letter) [rɪ'dʒekʃn]	Absage
relationship [rɪ'leɪʃnʃɪp]	Beziehung, Verhältnis
reliable [rɪ'laɪəbl]	zuverlässig
to **relocate** [ˌriːləʊ'keɪt]	umziehen/an einen anderen (Stand-)Ort ziehen
remuneration [rɪ,mjuːnə'reɪʃn]	Vergütung, Bezahlung
to **render** ['rendə]	zur Folge haben
to **report to** [rɪ'pɔːt tə]	(jdm) unterstellt sein/an (jdm) berichten
reporting relationship [rɪ,pɔːtɪŋ rɪ'leɪʃnʃɪp]	Stellung im Unternehmen
to **require** [rɪ'kwaɪə]	erfordern, erforderlich machen
requirement, practical ~ [ˌpræktɪkl rɪ'kwaɪəmənt]	praktische Anforderung
to **resign** [rɪ'zaɪn]	(Arbeitsstelle) kündigen (vom Arbeitnehmer/Angestellten ausgehend)
resignation [ˌrezɪg'neɪʃn]	Kündigung(sschreiben) (durch den Arbeitnehmer/Angestellten)
to **resolve** [rɪ'zɒlv]	lösen
respect, with ~ [wɪð rɪ'spekt]	bei allem Respekt
responsibility [rɪ,spɒnsə'bɪləti]	Verantwortung, Verpflichtung
responsible for [rɪ'spɒnsəbl fə]	verantwortlich für, zuständig für
responsible to [rɪ'spɒnsəbl tə]	(jdm) unterstellt
resumé ['rezjumeɪ]	Lebenslauf
to **retain** [rɪ'teɪn]	beschäftigen, beibehalten, erhalten
retirement scheme [rɪ'taɪəmənt skiːm]	(betriebliche) Alterversorgung
to **review** [rɪ'vjuː]	überprüfen
to **revise** [rɪ'vaɪz]	revidieren, überarbeiten
to **reward** [rɪ'wɔːd]	entlohnen
reward [rɪ'wɔːd]	Lohn, Vergütung
rise [raɪz]	(Gehalts-)Erhöhung
roughly ['rʌfli]	ungefähr, etwa
rumour ['ruːmə]	Gerücht
run, I've got to ~ [aɪv gɒt tə 'rʌn]	ich muss weg/gehen

S

to **sack** [sæk]	feuern, hinauswerfen
salary ['sæləri]	Gehalt, Lohn
salutation [ˌsælju'teɪʃn]	Anrede
satisfaction, to sb's ~ [ˌsætɪs'fæktʃn]	zu jds Zufriedenheit
satisfactory [ˌsætɪs'fæktəri]	zufriedenstellend, befriedigend
to **screen** [skri:n]	sichten, überprüfen
secondment ['sekəndmənt]	Versetzung, Einsatz an einem anderen (Stand-)Ort
secure [sɪ'kjuə]	sicher
to **see sb out** [ˌsi: 'aʊt]	jdn verabschieden
self-employed [ˌself ɪm'plɔɪd]	selbständig (arbeiten)
sensitive, to be ~ to [bi 'sensətɪv tə]	Rücksicht nehmen auf
sensitivity [ˌsensə'tɪvəti]	Sensibilität
to **settle in** [ˌsetl 'ɪn]	sich eingewöhnen, sich zurechtfinden
severe [sɪ'vɪə]	schwer
share [ʃeə]	(Geschäfts-)Anteil, Aktie
shift allowance [ʃɪft ə'laʊəns]	Schichtzuschlag
shift pattern ['ʃɪft pætn]	Schichtplan
shop floor [ˌʃɒp 'flɔ:]	Produktionsstätte, Werkstatt
shop steward [ˌʃɒp 'stjuːəd]	Mitglied des Betriebsrats, das einer Gewerkschaft angehört
shop, closed ~ [ˌkləʊzd 'ʃɒp]	gewerkschaftspflichtiger Betrieb
shop, open ~ [ˌəʊpən 'ʃɒp]	kein gewerkschaftspflichtiger Betrieb
to **shortlist** ['ʃɔːtlɪst]	in die engere Auswahl nehmen
sick leave ['sɪk li:v]	Genesungsurlaub, Zeit, in der jmd krankgeschrieben ist
sick pay provision [ˌsɪk peɪ prə'vɪʒn]	Krankengeld
sickness [ˌlɒŋ tɜːm 'sɪknəs]	Krankheit
to **slash** [slæʃ]	(drastisch) reduzieren
to **slip** [slɪp]	ausrutschen
sound knowledge [saʊnd 'nɒlɪdʒ]	fundierte Kenntnis(se)
staff [sta:f]	Angestellte, Personal
stakeholder pension [ˌsteɪkhəʊldə 'penʃn]	Rente aus Gewinnbeteiligung
to **strive** [straɪv]	bemüht sein
subject to ['sʌbdʒɪkt tə]	abhängig von
to **submit** [səb'mɪt]	einreichen, vorstellen
subsidiary [səb'sɪdiəri]	Tochter(gesellschaft)
to **subsidize** ['sʌbsɪdaɪz]	subventionieren
succession planning [sək'seʃn plænɪŋ]	Nachfolgeplanung
suggestion [sə'dʒestʃən]	Vorschlag
to **suit** [su:t]	passen
suitability [ˌsu:tə'bɪləti]	Eignung
suitable ['su:təbl]	geeignet, passend, angemessen
supervisor ['su:pəvaɪzə]	Abteilungsleiter/in
to **support** [sə'pɔ:t]	unterstützen
to **swap** [swɒp]	(aus)tauschen

T

to **take effect** [teɪk ɪ'fekt]	in Kraft treten
to **take on** [ˌteɪk 'ɒn]	übernehmen, einstellen
target ['ta:gɪt]	Ziel(vorgaben)
temporary employment [ˌtemprəri ɪm'plɔɪmənt]	Zeitarbeitsverhältnis

to **terminate** ['tɜːmɪneɪt]	(Vertrag) auflösen/beenden
threat ['θret]	Drohung
to **threaten** ['θretn]	drohen
time off in lieu [ˌtaɪm 'ɒf ɪn 'lu:]	Freizeit-, Zeitausgleich, Zeitgutschrift
tool [tu:l]	Instrument
touch wood [tʌtʃ 'wʊd]	toi, toi, toi
trade paper ['treɪd peɪpə]	Handelsblatt
trade press ['treɪd pres]	Handelsblätter
trade union [ˌtreɪd 'ju:niən]	Gewerkschaft
training audit [ˌtreɪnɪŋ 'ɔːdɪt]	Bestandsaufnahme für Training und Weiterbildung
training manual [ˌtreɪnɪŋ 'mænjuəl]	Handbuch zur Aus- und Weiterbildung
travelling expenses [ˌtrævlɪŋ ɪk'spensɪz]	(Reise-)Spesen, Reisekosten
trial period [ˌtraɪəl 'pɪəriəd]	Probezeit
to **trip** [trɪp]	stolpern

U

undersigned [ˌʌndə'saɪnd]	Unterzeichner/in
union rep(resentative) [ˌju:niən ˌreprɪ'zentətɪv]	Gewerkschaftsvertreter/in
unsociable hours [ʌn'səʊʃəbl 'aʊəz]	ungewöhnliche Arbeitszeiten
unsolicited application [ʌnsəˌlɪsɪtɪd ˌæplɪ'keɪʃn]	Initiativ-, Blindbewerbung
unsuccessful [ˌʌnsək'sesfl]	erfolglos
up to date, to be ~ [bi ˌʌp tə 'deɪt]	auf dem neuesten Stand sein
up to scratch [ˌʌp tə 'skrætʃ]	auf Vordermann
to **upset** [ʌp'set]	verwirren, aufregen

V

vacancy ['veɪkənsi]	offene Stelle
vacation (US) [və'keɪʃn]	Urlaub
to **value** ['vælju:]	schätzen
value ['vælju:]	Wert
victimization [ˌvɪktɪmaɪ'zeɪʃn]	Schikanierung, ungerechte Behandlung
vulnerable, to be ~ [bi 'vʌlnərəbl]	in einer prekären Lage sein

WY

wage differentials [weɪdʒ ˌdɪfə'renʃlz]	Lohnunterschiede
wage freeze ['weɪdʒ fri:z]	Lohnstopp
wage, minimum ~ [ˌmɪnɪməm 'weɪdʒ]	Mindestlohn
white-collar staff [ˌwaɪt 'kɒlə sta:f]	(Büro-)Angestellte
word of mouth [ˌwɜːd əv 'maʊθ]	Mundpropaganda
word, to have a ~ about [hæv ə 'wɜːd əbaʊt]	besprechen
work, pattern of ~ [ˌpætn əv 'wɜːk]	Arbeitszeiten
workforce ['wɜːkfɔːs]	Belegschaft
work-life balance [wɜːk 'laɪf 'bæləns]	Gleichgewicht zwischen Arbeit und Freizeit
workload ['wɜːkləʊd]	Arbeitsbelastung
workplace ['wɜːkpleɪs]	Arbeitsplatz
Would you mind ... ? [wʊd ju 'maɪnd]	Würde es Ihnen etwas ausmachen? Würden Sie bitte ...?
Yours sincerely [jɔːz sɪn'sɪəli]	Mit freundlichen Grüßen

Model letters

Business Systems Ltd

26 Lymington Road
Manchester M34 2RD
Tel: 0044 0675 23144
Fax: 0044 0675 23145
info@businesssystems.xyz.co.uk
www.businesssystems.xyz.co.uk

6 September 20..

Mr Heiko Fischer
Mouse Cottage
Green Lane
Sevenoaks Kent
TN15 2AP

Dear Mr Fischer

International Marketing Assistant – Manchester

Thank you for your letter of 2 September, applying for the position of International Marketing Assistant with this company.

We would like to invite you to attend an interview at this office and would be grateful if you could telephone the undersigned as soon as possible to arrange a suitable date and time. Enclosed is a copy of the person specification and job description for this job, which we would like you to familiarize yourself with before the interview. Alternatively, you can go to our website for these documents and other information about the company. A map showing the location of our office is also enclosed.

If you have any questions, please raise them when you call to arrange the interview.

We look forward to welcoming you to our offices.

Yours sincerely

John Spence

John Spence
Personnel Assistant

encs

A rejection letter

10 September 20..

Mr George McAllister
65 Belsize Lane
Belsize Village
London NW3 5AS

Dear Mr McAllister

International Marketing Assistant – Manchester

Thank you for your letter of 4 September, applying for the position of International Marketing Assistant recently advertised in *The Times*.

We have studied your curriculum vitae in depth, but regret that we are unable to offer you an interview at this time.

We wish you every success elsewhere and appreciate your interest in our company.

Yours sincerely

A rejection letter (after the first interview)

20 September 20..

Ms Alexandra Bang
Vester Voldgade 106
Copenhagen V
DK-1552 Denmark

Dear Ms Bang

International Marketing Assistant – Manchester

Thank you for attending the interview on 17 September for the above position. It was very nice meeting you.

We have now fully considered your application and regret that we are unable to offer you a second interview/the position on this occasion. We would like to reimburse you for your return flight to the interview and would ask you to send details of the cost, together with a receipt or copy of the ticket, and your bank details.

We will hold your details pending and let you know if a suitable opening occurs in the future.

We appreciate your interest in our company and would like to take this opportunity of wishing you every success elsewhere.

Yours sincerely

Business **S**ystems Ltd

26 Lymington Road
Manchester M34 2RD
Tel: 0044 0675 23144
Fax: 0044 0675 23145
info@businesssystems.xyz.co.uk
www.businesssystems.xyz.co.uk

20 September 20..

Mr Heiko Fischer
Mouse Cottage
Green Lane
Sevenoaks Kent
TN15 2AP

Dear Mr Fischer

International Marketing Assistant – Manchester

Further to your recent interviews, we have pleasure in offering you the position of
International Marketing Assistant in the UK Marketing Department, based at this
address, at a commencing salary of £30,000 per annum. This offer is conditional on
receiving a satisfactory reference from your present and last employers and to the
satisfactory completion of a three-month probationary period on either side.

Basic hours of work are normally 9 am to 6 pm Monday to Friday, including an hour
for lunch. It will be necessary for you to work overtime as and when required. Holiday
entitlement is 20 days per annum, rising to 25 after two years' service. Normally
holiday cannot be taken during the probationary period. All terms, conditions and
benefits are detailed in the handbook and contract enclosed.

We would like you to start on 1 November 20.., if possible. During your first week you
will participate in an induction seminar to familiarize you fully with the company. Full
details of this will be sent to you nearer the time.

Please let us know as soon as possible if you would like to accept by signing and
returning one copy of the contract. We will then take up references. We hope you will
join us and very much look forward to hearing from you.

Yours sincerely

June Stewart

June Stewart
Head of International HR

encs   Contract of employment
        Company handbook

Business Systems Ltd

26 Lymington Road
Manchester M34 2RD
Tel: 0044 0675 23144
Fax: 0044 0675 23145
info@businesssystems.xyz.co.uk
www.businesssystems.xyz.co.uk

25 September 20...

Glenda Martin
Human Resources Manager
Greenman International Books
25 Manning Avenue
Glasgow G23 6RT

Dear Ms Martin

Re: Heiko Fischer

The above-named is being considered for the post of International Marketing Assistant and has indicated that you would be willing to provide a reference. I should therefore be most grateful if you would confirm to me his position and the dates he was employed by your company.

It would also be helpful if you could clarify his sickness record over the last two years, as well as his reason for leaving your employment. Any information you can give as to Mr Fischer's suitability for the above type of position would be most helpful. I am enclosing a job description and person specification for the position he is being considered for.

Any information you provide will be treated in the strictest confidence and may I take this opportunity of thanking you in advance for any help you are able to give us. We would appreciate your prompt reply.

Yours sincerely

June Stewart

June Stewart
Head of International HR

encs

A reference

Greenman International Books

25 Manning Avenue • Glasgow G23 6RT
Tel: 0044 0141 628749 • Fax: 0044 0141 628750
www.GreenmanInt.co.uk

June Stewart
Head of International HR
Business Systems Ltd
26 Lymington Road
Manchester M34 2RD

28 September 20..

Dear Ms Stewart

Heiko Fischer

We refer to your letter of 25 September asking for a reference on behalf of the above.

Heiko Fischer was employed by this company from 1 January 1998 until 31 October 2004, when he left of his own accord. We understand he was proposing to travel for four months in Australia. He started as a trainee in our Public Relations department and transferred to Marketing in April 2000 where he worked as a Marketing Assistant. During his time in our employ he gave good service and worked to our satisfaction in all areas. His involvement in international affairs covered the last two years of his employment. During this period he had eight days' sickness recorded.

We are delighted to give a reference for Mr Fischer and have no reason to believe he would not be suitable for the job outlined in your enclosures. We wish him well in his future career. This reference is given without responsibility on the part of the writer and the company.

Yours sincerely

Glenda Martin

Glenda Martin
Human Resources Manager

Useful phrases and vocabulary

Job interviews

Establishing rapport and relaxing a candidate
It's nice to welcome you here and I hope you'll enjoy the interview.
Please feel free to ask any questions you may have.
I'm going to start by ... and then we'll talk about ... Finally, we can deal with any points you would like to raise.
Please ask about anything you are not sure of.

Giving information
I'd like to tell you something about ...
I'm afraid we don't ...
We'd be happy to ...
Let me fill you in on the details of ...

Questions
What experience have you had of ...?
What aspect of your job do you like best?
How would you handle ...?
How do you go about dealing with ...?
What do you know about managing ...?
Why do you want to leave your present job?
Could you outline your experience in ...?

Asking follow-up questions
Could you tell me more about ...?
What exactly do you mean by ...?
Could you enlarge on that?
I wonder if you could give me an example of ...
Why did you deal with the situation in that way?

Appraisal interviews

Questions
What do you like most about your work?
Could you tell me (how things are going with ...)?
How do you see (your team developing ...)?
Would you like to give me more details about ...?
When did you realize that ...?
Would you mind giving me more information on ...?
Is there anything else we should talk about?

Talking about problems
I'd like you to tell me (how you see your progress over the last year).
Has there been anything you have found difficult to cope with?
How are things with the rest of the department?
Have there been any problems?
Could there be a (personality) problem between ...?
Why weren't you able to talk about it?

Softening disagreement
With respect, I think ...
To be quite frank, I don't think ...
(I'm) Not sure I agree with you there.
Frankly, we should deal with that differently ...
I respect your opinion, but ...
I'm afraid we can't .../I'm sorry but we can't ...
To a certain extent I agree, but ...

Negotiating

Persuading
It would be to your advantage to ...
It might be in your interest to ...
We can reassure you on that point totally.
It's the best offer around. You won't find a better one.
I was wondering if you had any thoughts about ...?
Wouldn't it be an excellent idea if ...?

Bargaining and compromising
We could consider (doing) that if you promised to ...?
How would it look if we offered ...?
Sorry, we've already had a better offer, so ...
We would agree on one condition: ...
Our pay deal is conditional on ...
If you agree to ..., we can ...
If you threaten us, we'll withdraw the offer.
If we had to ..., it's unlikely we could ...
We might put a better offer on the table, provided (that) you ...
I'd go along with that on condition that you returned to work.
Unless you return to work, we'll withdraw our offer.
That seems a good compromise, as long as there is ...

Arranging an appointment

What date would be convenient for you?
What time would suit you?
Would Monday at 10.30 suit you?
Is the 5th of March at 6 pm convenient?
Can you manage …?/How about …?
Tuesday would be good for me.
Monday's bad for me, I'm afraid.
That sounds fine.
Yes, that would be good for me.
I think that should be possible.

Exchanging information

Can we just have a word about …?
I'd like to be kept up to date on what's happening.
So where/what are you planning to …?
Well, firstly I thought I would …
I'll look into it (though).

Asking for somebody's opinion or ideas

What is your view on this?
Could I have some feedback?
Could I have your input?
Could you please prepare a summary …?

Giving an opinion or feedback

Good idea./That's fine.
As far as I'm concerned …
It seems to me that …/In my opinion …
Why don't we …?
Well, I'm definitely in favour of …
By the way, shouldn't we …?

Agreeing and disagreeing

I entirely agree.
Yes, (that's a) good idea.
I'm inclined to agree with you on that.
Yes, but have you considered …?
You have a point there, but …
I'm afraid I can't go along with that.
Sorry, but I really can't agree.

Making recommendations and suggestions

We need to introduce …
My proposal is to put …
Maybe we should also look into …
I recommend introducing/that we introduce …
It's essential that we take up references …
I (can) recommend talking/that we talk …
It's high time (that) we introduced …
I suggest we might …
What do you think about …?
I believe we should consider …

Clarifying

Could you repeat that?
Sorry, I didn't quite get that.
What exactly do you mean by …?
As you know, we really do need to …
I'll fill you in on …

Interrupting

Could I just say that …?
I'd like to add a point here.
Excuse me, can I just come in here?

Key HR word families

verb	noun (person)	noun (object/concept)	adjective/adverb
to **apply**	applicant	application	applicable
to **appraise**	appraisor appraisee	appraisal	
to **assess**	assessor	assessment	
to **benefit**	beneficiary	benefit	beneficial(ly)
to **consult**	consultant	consultancy consultation	consulting
to **employ** to reemploy	employer employee	(un)employment (in sb's) employ	self-employed (un)employed (un)employable
to **equal**		(in)equality	(in)equal/equally
(to be **flexible**)		flexibility flexitime/flextime	(in)flexible/flexibly
to **negotiate**	negotiator	negotiation	negotiable
to **recruit**	recruit recruiter	recruitment	
to **select**		selection	selective(ly)